Newcastle
& Tyneside
THE GOLDEN YEARS

CONTENTS

First designed and published in Great Britain by True North Books Limited
England HX3 6SN
01422 244555
www.truenorthbooks.com
Copyright © True North Books Limited, 2013

INTRODUCTION

For all of us, memories are the currency which we use to record the changes and progress in our everyday lives and to fix our place as individuals in the greater scheme of things. This is the latest publication in our 'Memories' series of publications, covering nostalgic reflections of towns and cities throughout the UK. In this new book we will be meandering through a pictorial cross-section of life in Newcastle and Tyneside over the last 100 years or so, to help satisfy the longing we all get from time to time, to recall wistful memories of a different era that now seems better or simpler.

As we get older it is often easier to take a step back, and to view events and developments with a clearer sense of prospective. Our aim has been to assist in this respect by presenting a publication relevant to the area capable of rekindling memories of days gone by in an entertaining and informative manner. Looking through the pages of this book it is interesting to reflect on exactly how much change has taken place in Newcastle and Tyneside over a relatively short period, relative to the long history of the area dating back to the Domesday Book of 1086.

Many of these photographs are quite unique and will inevitably remind us of experiences and events in our lives, of our families and of those whose influence and support has touched us to a

greater or lesser degree. Whilst regret and loss play a part in our development as individuals, we sincerely hope this generic and random glimpse of the region, through photographs and interesting captions, will also trigger the odd smile and a warm glow associated with nostalgic memories from the past.

Defining features about nostalgia are universal and can bring back fond memories from a time gone by. Recent research shows that nostalgia can counteract loneliness, boredom and anxiety. Couples feel closer and look happier when they're sharing nostalgic memories. People generally get a 'Warm Glow' inside when relating to events and occasions in the past and enjoy reminiscences about how things used to be – even when these events sometimes have a painful side. When people speak wistfully of the past, they typically become more optimistic and inspired about the future.

We can all remember events surrounding friends and family, holidays, weddings, special occasions and nights out in Newcastle. So let your mind wander and think of the youthful days at the dance hall or courting in one of the many cinemas in the city. Be entertained as we take you on a sentimental journey through the pages of 'Newcastle & Tyneside – The Golden Years'…. Happy Memories!

TEXT — STEVE AINSWORTH, ANDREW MITCHELL, BRENDAN O'NEILL, TONY LAX

PHOTOGRAPH RESEARCH — TONY LAX, BRENDAN O'NEILL

DESIGNER — SEAMUS MOLLOY

BUSINESS DEVELOPMENT MANAGER — PETER PREST

VICTORIAN & EDWARDIAN TIMES

This page: Pictured around 1880, the organ grinder was getting ready to entertain passers-by with the tunes coming from his barrel organ and the antics of the monkey he used to collect contributions from those who enjoyed the performance. He was one of a number of street buskers and performers who earned a living from the generosity of others. Some of the entertainers offered a fairly repetitive repertoire, but that did not matter much as the clientele was transient. The grinder kept a watchful eye out for the police who were often keen to move him on. Along with his monkey, usually a capuchin, he might now be regarded as the forerunner of the 21st century street beggar with his seemingly ever-present dog. But, at least the organ grinder tried to be entertaining rather than demanding. However, not everyone liked the show. George Orwell, a generation later, wrote on the subject that, 'it is perfectly legal to annoy one's fellow citizens by pretending to entertain them with dreadful music'.

Right: Mrs Richardson had her fruit seller's pitch outside Newcastle Central Station. Her family could well have been using this spot for 50 years, as the station opened in 1850. By the turn of the century, when this determined looking woman was photographed, the line through here was a well-established route linking London with the two major Scottish cities. The subject of the image had a hard job, though, drumming up custom as the majority of people passing her stall were more interested in getting home or being on time to catch their train than in buying fruit.

Top left: In the early part of the 20th century, motorcycles were little more than cycles with a motor, hence the name. It was not until later that bikes that were recognisably related to the modern motorcycle became generally available on the British market. The French Werner helped to pioneer the conventional position of the engine in place of the bicycle's bottom bracket and many British manufacturers had their own variations on the theme. Many of these early bikes were too primitive and too demanding to appeal to anyone but committed and well-heeled enthusiasts. Although the engines were relatively low powered, the lightweight chassis helped to give these machines reasonable performance - for the time. Here we can see Mr W Elder of Newcastle in 1908, proudly showing off his new machine. The well-tried 3½ hp bike could be had in three modes, tourist with direct belt drive, de luxe with roc clutch only, or with clutch and two-speed gear.

Left: On 20 July, 1898, this troupe of ladies performed a neat routine at the Gosforth Rural Fete. With a musical accompaniment behind them, the female cyclists demonstrated a routine of synchronised movement for the entertainment of an appreciative crowd. Despite being handicapped by their long skirts, as it would have been far too racy to show a leg or even an ankle, the display of two-wheeled skill was carried out magnificently. Cycling had become very popular with women. It gave them the opportunity to get out and about, as well as to exercise and indulge in a sport, without the need of chaperones or maiden aunts to keep them in check. It was this sort of attempt to show an independent spirit that helped underpin Mrs Pankhurst's activities in pursuing women's rights.

Above: The photograph from the beginning of the last century, could be entitled 'Swan Lake'. This very well dressed little girl seems particularly interested in the swan, whilst the two matriarchal ladies stand and watch. The photograph shows the edge of the lake in Brandling Park, Jesmond. The lake was a popular spot in summer as children were allowed to go paddling, which probably meant the swans got no peace.

enerations of Tyneside poor knew these scenes from the famed Paddy's Market, on the Quayside. Here, anything useful in the clothing line was bartered or sold, including cast-off clothes, shoes, boots, ties and ribbons that went on sale every week. Re-cycling society's left-overs was the name of the game and these Victorian ladies in the picture below were playing a vital role in the lives of their customers. Although it is thought that the Paddy's market was started in the early Victorian years by Irish people bought over to break the miners' strike, in truth, the trade has always existed. This practice continued into the second half of the 20th Century. Some people may recall being told to tidy their room because it looked like "Paddy's market"

In 1905, the King Edward VII Bridge was roughly half built. It would be completed the following year. It was designed by C A Harrison, the senior engineer for the North Eastern Railway. Built by the Cleveland Bridge and Engineering Company from Darlington, it has an interesting design of four lattice steel spans that rest on concrete piers. The King himself, accompanied by Queen Alexandra, performed the ceremonial opening ceremony on 10 July, 1906. It is just one of many bridges across the Tyne that are icons of this part of England.

ENTERTAINMENT LEISURE & PASTIMES

All the fun of the fair, a series of photographs from the 'Hoppings', the first dating back over 100 years to 1906. It had an atmosphere all of its own that had to be experienced to be appreciated. In its heyday, figures recorded suggest that over a million visitors attended the Town Moor festival, to spend their Race Week leisure time and hard-earned cash over several days of summer sunshine. The Hoppings was Europe's largest travelling fairground and was held on the Town Moor for the last full week in June for 130 years. The fair began as a

Temperance Fair in 1882. It was scheduled to coincide with Race Week at Newcastle Racecourse during which the Northumberland Plate was awarded. It had over 60 large rides and many more children's rides and stalls - everything from roller coasters and funhouses to teacups and big wheels, and was a must-see spectacle for Geordies and visitors alike.

Several origins have been suggested for the name. Most relate to dancing, the word "hopping" meaning a dance in Middle English (Old fairs included dancing). Another idea stems from the clothing which the travellers used to wear; that being of old, sack like tops and pants. Clothing often became infested with fleas from the animals that travelled with the fair. People were often seen "jumping" or "hopping" about itching from the bites they received. Or the name may derive from the Anglo-Saxon word "hoppen" meaning funfair.

Who could forget the noise and excitement of the Hoppings? The whirr and hum of the rides, the loud beat of the music, several different tunes fighting with each other for attention, the shouts of the man who bravely volunteered to guess your weight, and the squeals of the girls as they rose to the top of the big wheel. And the food! The toffee apples, dark red and shining as if they have been varnished, the paper bags of crunchy brandy snap and the ice cream, in tubs, cornets or wafers, and the shocking pink candy floss. Remember the time when it was sold from booths where it was spun around a stick while you waited? The sterile, pre-bagged confection we buy today bears little resemblance to the real thing - after all, sticky fingers were all part of the day's fun! Its hundreds of amusements, rides and stalls covered around 30 acres. In days gone by, of course, the rides were all steam driven, from the merry-go-rounds to the swing boats that closely resembled the Riverboat.

The Hoppings is a much looked-forward-to event, and by the end of every April excitement is already building up, especially among the younger members of the family. Since the 1960s the rides at the Hoppings have become progressively more sophisticated; contrast the 127ft Liberty Wheel that visited the Hoppings for the first time in 1995 with the big wheel of former days! The Big Wheel has been in existence as long as any swings or roundabouts, and has remained unchanged in basic design principles. Great Wheels were built for early exhibitions such as Earls Court (1894) with machines such as this capable of carrying 1,200 passengers within its 40 carriages. Production of travelling Big Wheels began between the wars, with initially 16 car machines opening, followed by a more portable 12 car version. The recent trend has been for Giant Wheels once again, with the London Eye proving a fine example of a classic idea.

In the above photograph it was all the fun of the fair at the Temperance Festival towards the end of the 1930s. These young men were keen to demonstrate their dodgem driving skills, just as their grandchildren might do today. Some fairground attractions have not changed over the years. The drivers photographed here, however, might soon have changed their vehicles from these recreational ones to those with a real purpose. In September of the following year, war was declared and men such as these were soon to be behind the wheel of a tank or army truck.

The Temperance Festival had, in itself, been started as a revival of former annual gatherings that had taken place in earlier times when locals joined forces to have fun. Those behind the festival's existence saw it as a counter attraction to the summer race meeting that took place each year at Gosforth Park. Sober citizens regarded this as a venue that often encouraged drunkenness and debauchery. Having a good time without resorting to demon drink as an aid was a popular move in late Victorian England, especially with families. The fair soon became well established and, looking at this 1938 scene, you might say that it went helter skelter on a successful journey.

These two images from the hopping are post war. We can bet that this little madam was not as shy as she was pretending. Posing with mum in 1957, she was enjoying a go on the roundabout. In theory it is possible to plot the progress of fairground ride development through the 19th century until, roughly, 1914 and the outbreak of World War I. During this period it was all essentially swings and roundabouts. The advent of electical power and the innovative technology that came with it changed all this and rides became more varied, with more and more manufacturers entering the market as the leisure industry expanded.Funfairs are seen as family entertainment, and most include a significant number of children's rides. Many of these are smaller, platform based rides like, cup & saucer, toysets, train rides then there are smaller slower versions of the adult rides, Ferris wheels, waltzers, even children's bumper cars.

The Hoppings was crowded with early 1960s' revellers enjoying themselves at the funfair. All the traditional stalls were there, such as coconut shies with the objects seemingly glued on tight, rifle ranges that had guns with off centre sights and hoopla using rings that nearly fitted over the prizes. We all knew we would waste our money, but it was fun doing so. The fairground rides were just great. Noble's provided many of them. This was, and still is, a well known name in this part of England. It is presently on its seventh generation of family owners and boasts a history going back to late Victorian times. Rather sadly, the Council removed funding for The Hoppings in 2013 and replaced it with a fair of its own. The future for the traditional festival is difficult to determine.

I t started life in medieval times and was once a bustling gathering place where shoppers could bag a bargain. The Bigg Market lay beyond the narrow markets, with the road narrowing as it progressed to become Newgate Street. Today, Newcastle's oldest and smallest market, the Bigg Market, is a shadow of its former self. No longer do dozens of stalls line the streets offering families cheap fruit, vegetables and freshly baked bread. The name 'Bigg' refers to

a type of coarse barley that used to be sold in this market. It was one of a cluster of markets along what was then the Great North Road, which crossed the Tyne under the protection of the castle and through the town to the New Gate before turning north along what is now Percy Street.

Above: Golf and football seem to have gone hand in hand over the years. Hitting a ball down the fairway was a good form of athletic relaxation for Newcastle United players on their day off or after a morning's gentle training. It was a far better pursuit than heading off to the billiard hall, down to the race track or across the road to the pub. Bob Thomson was a Scottish international fullback who joined United from arch rivals Sunderland, playing 80 games before moving to Hull City. He cut a natty figure on the golf course, somewhat removed from the rugged way he played his main sport.

Bottom left: In 1955, British hopes of success in competitive play centred upon Max Faulkner, Henry Cotton, Dai Rees and the young Peter Alliss. Their respective merits were discussed in between shots by the members of Gosforth Park Golf Club. Then the conversation moved on to descriptions of shots and holes they had played ages ago. They could talk you through every stroke, that is if you were not too busy boring the pants off playing partners with your own talk of lipped putts and errant drives.

Below: Children enjoying themselves are timeless. This scene could be drawn from any part of the last century, but it is in fact one from The Hoppings in the summer of 1930. It is difficult to believe that the land was in the grip of the early years of the biggest industrial depression our nation had ever experienced. These kiddies look so carefree in their fancy dress outfits. If only we could always shelter them from that careworn world out there. At the same time, one supposes, we have to help them deal with difficulty, but how we wish we could keep them at this level of innocence for ever and a day.

Above: The Spanish City was a permanent funfair in Whitley Bay. Erected as a smaller version of Blackpool's Pleasure Beach, it opened in 1910 as a concert hall, restaurant, roof garden and tearoom. A ballroom was added in 1920 and later the funfair. Early attractions included the Social Whirl (giving way to the Water Chute seen in this photograph), Rainbow Pleasure Wheel, Figure 8 Railway, River Caves, the House That Jack Built, the Joy Wheel, a fairy castle and an Indian Jungle. When paid holidays became common in the fifties, hordes of Scottish workers and their families descended on Whitley Bay during Glasgow Fairs Week with factories closed for the annual holidays. Hundreds of coaches arrived and Station Road was a solid mass of people with trains running very frequently.

Left: By 1930, girls were being encouraged to indulge in more active pastimes than those to which their mums and grannies had been restricted. After all, how could you practise netball, play hockey or go ice skating in long, flowing Edwardian dresses or Victorian crinolines? There was also the influence of emancipation in this scene at Gosforth School. The struggles of the Suffragettes and the wartime experiences of women on the factory floor helped change attitudes and activities. Girls were literally no longer straitlaced.

Right: A busy scene looking along Pilgrim Street in 1947. Even though petrol rationing was still in force, the road is crammed with traffic and the pedestrians appear to be taking a risk crossing in front of the vehicles. On the right we can make out the Odeon Cinema, which originally opened as The Paramount in September 1931. It was one of only seven Paramount Theatre's built by the American owned Paramount Theatres Ltd. in cities in the UK. The Paramount was sumptuous inside, with a fan shaped seating area for 2,600 customers. On November 27, 1939, all the Paramount theatres were sold to Odeon and the Newcastle venue was renamed in 1940. A plan to demolish and redevelop the site in 1972 came to nothing and in 1975 the venue was tripled. Good years followed – the cinema survived an AMC multiplex opening in 1987 and a major refurbishment was carried out. Sadly, it closed in 2002 and now stands empty and unused.

We would normally expect Queen Elizabeth the Queen Mother to be more at home on the racecourse than on the bowling green. But this delightful photograph from 1936 when she was the Duchess of York shows her in relaxed and happy mood as she confidently launches a wood across a Tyneside bowling green. Her Majesty was just 36 years of age when the picture was taken, over seventy five years ago. She was accompanying her husband, The Duke of York, later King George VI, on a tour of the North East.

Right: Tate's Radio had premises at 95 Grainger Street and 50a New Bridge Street and, as its name suggests, grew up in the age of the wireless when families would gather round their sets in the living room to enjoy the delights of Henry Hall or ITMA coming over the airwaves. In the early 1950s there were great serials like 'Journey into space' and that forerunner of modern soap operas, 'The Archers'. We chuckled at the antics of the Goons and the Clitheroe Kid and even accepted the now crazy idea that Peter Brough, a ventriloquist, should have a radio show with his dummy Archie Andrews. But, as television began to invade our lives, Tate's and its contemporaries had to tool up its workshops to deal with the new phenomenon. It was Queen Elizabeth's

coronation that seemed to kick start a medium that had been struggling to get a foothold in our homes. Many of us watched the ceremony on a friend's flickering black and white set and were immediately hooked. Having bought a TV outright, or perhaps on hire purchase, we got full value for our money, even sitting through a picture of a potter's wheel during an interlude in transmission. Even BBC radio took note, killing off Grace Archer, one of its most popular characters, on the night that ITV was launched in an effort to pinch the limelight.

Below "Uncle Andy" the toy man is at the kerbside displaying his Christmas fare. Andy Bell, of Benwell, was "uncle" to hundreds of kiddies in the area. Each afternoon his little black van was packed to the roof with dolls, train sets, blackboards, modeling sets, mouth organs and everything the toddlers could wish for. This photograph shows the excited children sitting on the road behind "Uncle Andy's" van in October 1949. It is refreshing to see the children so happy and engrossed, but this is clearly an image of the time and is unlikely to be repeated today.

A Sunday Market has been held on the Quayside for hundreds of years - the city's historical records refer to it as far back as 1736, and it was probably in existence long before then. Three of Newcastle's famous bridges make a stunning background to the view as hundreds of punters browse among the stalls hoping to pick up a bargain. The children, of course, have their eye on the helium filled balloons that still have as much pull today as they did when a photographer captured this charming view. Slick-talking salesmen have always been around to charm the pennies and shillings from people's pockets, and whatever was on offer that day, a few pound notes or even fivers were no doubt handed over by punters eager to part with their cash.

The original Quayside market stretched from the old Tyne Bridge (near the site of the current Swing Bridge) along Sandgate and beyond. Commercial stalls selling every manner of goods were pitched along the riverside with a variety of fairground attractions strongmen, escapologists, and racing tipsters providing added entertainment. This photograph of Newcastle's quayside market was taken in 1964. Today, a weekend market is still held on the quayside, carrying on the city's long history of market trading. Over the centuries many different types of market have been held in the city, some such as the Bigg Market and Hay Market have lent their names to areas of the city

Right: If you think that women's football is something modern, think again. There was such a thing in a time before Rachel Yankey laced up a pair of boots, as we can see from this picture taken just before kick off in a match between the North of England and Scotland, played on 12 June, 1938. The Quaker Ladies, a team from Darlington, represented our interests. Here, one of the visiting XI is getting a massage before she crosses the touchline to do battle with the 'auld enemy'. Women's football became very popular during the 1914-18 War. Many sides drew their players from the largely female workforce in munitions factories. It started to lose popularity in the 1920s, though some charity games were played. Even so, in 1927, Darlington Quaker Ladies was founded, largely in an effort to raise funds to help the

mining community. The club continued to play occasional games throughout the 1930s in front of crowds numbering several thousands, despite opposition from the misogynist FA that obstructed women's football at every turn.

Left: This view, completely dominated by men in hats and caps, is taken at Brandling Park about 1955. Like many City parks, Brandling was recovered from the Town Moor, "redeemed from very unpromising surroundings and its present condition reflects the highest credit on the public-spirited action of the corporation". The Park was completed in 1878. The Brandling family (after whom the park was named) played a leading role in Newcastle life for 450 years. They acted as mayors, businessmen, M.Ps, landowners and mine owners. It was the disastrous explosion at the Brandling's Felling Colliery in 1812 that led to the invention of the miner's safety lamp.

Brandling and Exhibition Parks are situated in the two different wards of South Jesmond and Wingrove separated only by the A1, which has a lit public underpass giving access from one park to the other. They are both formal parks with attractive gardens. Brandling Park, the smaller of the two, is situated to the east of the A1 with Clayton Road being to the north boundary of the park. The women get their opportunity as there are both ladies and men's clubs on the side of the Bowling Green.

Above: Exhibition Park, redeveloped in 2013-14, has a long history dating back into the 19th century. Plans had been made in the 1870s to provide open space for public enjoyment and a sum of £2,000 was set aside to achieve this in the 1880s. However, a request was made for a larger parcel of land to be used so that Queen Victoria's Golden Jubilee could be properly marked with a grand exhibition. Land on and around Bull Park was made available and the Royal Exhibition was held, attracting over 2,000,000 visitors. Exhibition Park is the legacy of that event, though the bandstand is the only remaining structure from that time. The view across the lake dates from just over 50 years ago.

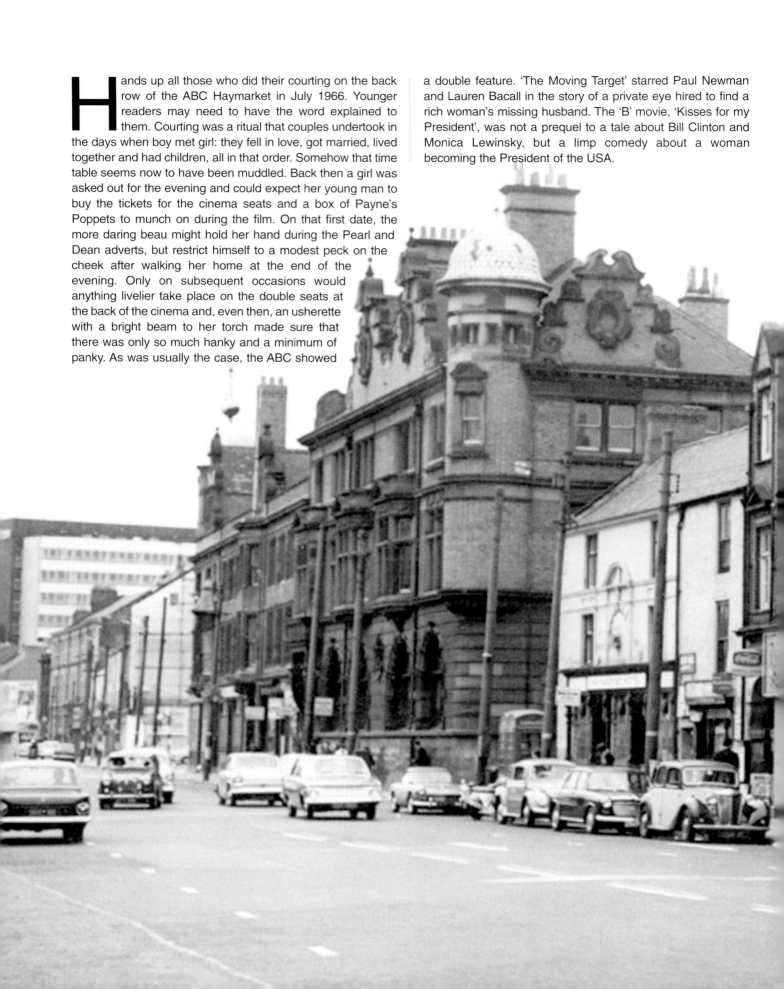

Hands up all those who did their courting on the back row of the ABC Haymarket in July 1966. Younger readers may need to have the word explained to them. Courting was a ritual that couples undertook in the days when boy met girl: they fell in love, got married, lived together and had children, all in that order. Somehow that time table seems now to have been muddled. Back then a girl was asked out for the evening and could expect her young man to buy the tickets for the cinema seats and a box of Payne's Poppets to munch on during the film. On that first date, the more daring beau might hold her hand during the Pearl and Dean adverts, but restrict himself to a modest peck on the cheek after walking her home at the end of the evening. Only on subsequent occasions would anything livelier take place on the double seats at the back of the cinema and, even then, an usherette with a bright beam to her torch made sure that there was only so much hanky and a minimum of panky. As was usually the case, the ABC showed a double feature. 'The Moving Target' starred Paul Newman and Lauren Bacall in the story of a private eye hired to find a rich woman's missing husband. The 'B' movie, 'Kisses for my President', was not a prequel to a tale about Bill Clinton and Monica Lewinsky, but a limp comedy about a woman becoming the President of the USA.

was helped by the opening of the North Tyne Loop railway line in 1882, connecting the coastal villages to Newcastle. The line followed the route of the present Metro line, and necessitated the building of a new railway station in the centre of the town, as well as another at Monkseaton. Both stations are still in use as Metro stations.

The town was known as Whitley until the 1890s, by which time the confusion of the name with Whitby, in North Yorkshire, was often causing mail to be misdirected. So the story goes, the final straw came in September 1901 when an ex-resident died in Edinburgh and his body was to be buried in St Paul's churchyard, Whitley. Unfortunately, the body was transported to Whitby by mistake causing the funeral to be delayed. The council asked residents for suggestions for a new name, and the most popular choice was Whitley Bay. It has since been known as Whitley Bay, but many residents still refer to the town as 'Whitley'.

Whitley Bay is a seaside town on the North Sea coast and has a fine golden sandy beach forming a bay stretching from St. Mary's Island in the north to Cullercoats in the south. From the late 19th century and into the 20th century the adverse effects of the decline of local coalmining and dependent industries in the area were largely improved by the emergence of Whitley as a seaside holiday resort. Its popularity with holidaymakers

Dire Straits songwriter Mark Knopfler said in a television interview that the Spanish City held special significance for him as the first place he ever heard loud rock 'n' roll. Dire Straits refer to it in their 1980 song "Tunnel of Love". For years the song was the unofficial theme song for the fairground, played every morning when the park opened. Even Sting (Gordon Sumner), who was born near Newcastle, wrote in his memoirs that he whiled away afternoons and evenings in the Spanish City's amusement arcades when he should have been studying for his A levels.

Just yards from the seafront, the Spanish City had a 180 ft-long Renaissance-style frontage, and became known for its distinctive dome, believed to have been the second-largest unsupported concrete dome in the UK when it was built, now a Grade 2 listed building. The building's architects were Robert Burns Dick, Charles T. Marshall, and James Cackett.

Still today, it is a popular place for recreation and is regularly used by walkers. The promenade and The Links have wonderful walks with the beach as a magnificent backdrop. In the lively photograph below, taken in the summer of 1959, a number of girls appearing at the Empire Theatre in Newcastle are photographed enjoying themselves on the beach at Whitley Bay or is it 'Whitley'?

The new pleasure palace was formally opened by Robert Mason, chair of the local council, on 7 May, 1910, and was called The Spanish City and Whitley Bay Pleasure Gardens. The Union Jack was flown at half mast because King Edward VII had died the previous day. The new building housed the 1400-capacity Empress theatre with a seating capacity of 1,400 on the floor and 400 on the balcony. There were also shops, cafes and roof gardens. The Empress Ballroom was added in 1920, and the Rotunda in 1921. The funfair was extremely popular, with fairground rides and amusements, including a "corkscrew" roller coaster , ghost train and waltzers, the House that Jack Built, and the Fun House. Historically, Whitley Bay became a holiday destination for the people of North East England and Scotland and remained popular in this regard until the 1980s.

Above: The Newcastle Diamonds race on the speedway track at the Brough Park Stadium on Fossway in Byker. The first meeting here took place in 1929, with an admission price of threepence, not much more than a penny in today's money. This form of racing quickly became very popular up and down the country. The noise of the bikes and the smells associated with cinder track speedway saw crowds flock in their thousands to meetings every weekend. In the early days, riders were so well known that their faces appeared on cigarette cards. One such image was of Gordon Byers who was just 17 when he won the inaugural race at Brough Park. In later times, men who would be world champions took to the saddle for the Diamonds. Ivan Mauger, Ole Olsen, Anders Michanek and Nicki Pedersen all rode for us.

Right: This fascinating view was captured in December 1981 as the concert-goers gathered outside the City Hall and formed an orderly queue that stretched around the building. They are queuing to see Lindisfarne, a British folk rock and progressive rock band from Newcastle, established in 1970. The group began as 'The Downtown Faction', led by Rod Clements, but soon changed their name to Brethren. In 1968, they were joined by Alan Hull and became Lindisfarne after the island of that name off the coast of Northumberland. The annual concert has been an institution in Newcastle ever since the long ago days when the group made 'Fog on the Tyne' a national hit. Closer inspection of the photograph reveals that the majority of people in the shot are young people intent on enjoying their Christmas treat. The Lindisfarne Christmas Concert was an established tradition which was carried on even after the tragic death of Alan Hull, until the group finally broke up, performing a final concert on 1 November, 2003. Ten years later, in support of Newcastle City Hall which was then under threat of closure, Ray Jackson announced he would return with Lindisfarne to the iconic venue for a Christmas show for the first time in 23 years and tickets sold out within hours.

Right: Pigeon fancying is a great northern tradition. These chaps, seen some 50 years ago, had no time for Eric Burdon and his Animals. Their creatures had wings, not songs about houses in New Orleans. Pigeon lofts in back yards were almost akin to churches as places of worship for some folk. Of course, these noble birds also played a major part in wartime, carrying messages from the frontlines or from special agents behind them. In 1943, the first three awards of the Dickin Medal, the gallantry order given to animals, went to pigeons. White Vision, Winkie and Tyke all delivered messages that helped rescue ditched aircrews.

M arkets have always played an important part in the life of the people of Newcastle. Grainger Market is situated between the New Gate of the old Town Walls and the newly laid out Grainger Street. Richard Grainger, builder and developer, planned and constructed some of Newcastle's finest buildings and streets during the 1830s. It was opened in front of a crowd of some 2,000

local people. The market revolutionised shopping in its day. When it opened it was the largest indoor market in the world. At the time of its opening in 1835 it was considered the most spacious and magnificent market in Europe and the 'Evening Chronicle' described it as 'the most beautiful in the world'. Now a Grade I listed building, there are plenty of stalls with fresh produce from a wide range of butchers, greengrocers and fishmongers. Hidden within is the unique 'Marks and Spencer Original Penny Bazaar', the world's smallest Marks & Spencer store. The Grainger Market is one of the few remaining the 19th century covered markets still trading as a market.

The featured couple below are firm fashion followers of 1970s' style. The flared trousers, platform shoes and United scarves tied to their wrists, á la Bay City Rollers, are a dead giveaway.

Looking along Raby Street from Priory Place, with Mason Street to the right, all this part of Byker has been redeveloped since this 1975 photograph was taken. The crumbling roadway and tired housing are no more. However, the replacements are not particularly inspiring. Although the road had tarmac laid, it soon became potholed. The replacement homes are a mix of low cost housing and low level flats, set in a rather cramped area. Byker is a district that has suffered from the sort of social problems seen in many comparable inner city areas. This part of Newcastle became known nationally, thanks to the teens' TV programme 'Byker Grove'. Because of that show that we now see Ant McPartlin regularly on our screens. Thanks indeed.

MASON ST.

6

Mary Bigot Slack who had a vision of an organisation in which women could renew their energy on a daily basis. She had a total belief in the power of the fairer sex to make the world a better place. In the 1930s, sports fields and church halls were full of ladies in shorts and vests, performing what would later be known as aerobics in group demonstrations of fitness and dexterity. Somewhat ironically, Slack died in 1935 at the tender age of just 50, but her legacy of a healthy body helping create a healthy mind lived on.

Above: This was the beginning of the swinging 60s but these young ladies, members of the Newcastle Keep Fit Club, were more interested in watching their Indian clubs on the move than with racier activities. Keeping in trim in this way had its roots in the Women's League of Health and Beauty founded in 1930 by

Below: Is this the next Beryl Burton? Long before the success of Victoria Pendleton and the British cycling team, these ladies at the Elite Ladies Cycling Club in Newcastle are out posing for a photograph. Although obviously

enjoying themselves, there seems to be a distinct lack of bikes in this image from the 1980s. The Elite Ladies are Win Massingale, Mary McLane, Doris Caldcleugh, Doreen Newton (on the bike), Lucy Anderson, Maisie Taylor, Molly Grey and Margaret Jackson. For our younger readers, Beryl Burton was one of Britain's greatest ever athletes, who dominated women's cycle racing in the UK. She won more than 90 domestic championships and seven world titles and set numerous national records.

Above: Elswick became part of Newcastle in 1835. Before long, its population had grown tremendously, changing it from a hamlet into a small town. Coal mining, Armstrong's armaments factor and the coming of the railways all helped swell the influx of new blood to the area in Victorian times. Elswick Park, opened in 1881 in the grounds formerly belonging to Elswick Hall, was once the site of a priory. As time went by, the recreational facilities were in dire need of attention. Refurbishment of the grounds included the building of a new swimming pool. It was completed by 20 January, 1981, almost a century after the park was opened to the public. Local children are seen here enjoying their first dip in the new facility as various dignitaries enjoy getting into the picture if not the water.

EVENTS & OCCASIONS

Excessive downpours have proved to be the problem in both these photographs, which are almost 30 years apart. The oldest picture, with the two young boys elping to clean up, is taken around the start of the First World War. An extraordinary deluge caused floods and landslips and there were several lightning fatalities. A second image from 1941 shows Chatsworth Gardens, Westerhope, under water during the floods. In the foreground two boys are rowing a homemade boat across the street. The flash flood of 22 June, 1941 was not recorded in the papers at the time due to war restrictions. However, the published 'British Rainfall' notes that a succession of severe thunderstorms passed over Newcastle that afternoon. Between 1425 GMT and 1645 GMT there was a total of 113mm of rain with 95mm falling in just 85 minutes. There was considerable hail damage in the district, with the area of greatest intensity recorded to the west and north of the city centre from Gosforth to Denton Burn.

Above and top right: Held five years after the British Empire Exhibition in London, and at the start of the Great Depression, the North East Coast Exhibition was intended to encourage local heavy industry. It was a symbol of pride and industrial success of the region and at the same time an advertisement for local industry and commerce. It was opened on by the then Prince of Wales (later Edward VII) in what is now Newcastle's Exhibition Park. Attractions included a Palace of Engineering, a Himalayan Railway, and an African Village! In these two photographs, we can see the main promenade of the exhibition, and a rare image of the Prince enjoying the Merry-go-Round. When it closed on 26 October, 1929, over four million people had attended (with an average of 30,000 visitors per day), and when the pavilions were dismantled the area reverted to a public park. Gold watches were given to each one-millionth visitor.

Below: In 1930, there was great unrest in the land. Rallies such as this one brought workers together as union leaders and activists spoke out about the poor pay and conditions that were their lot. Some of those on poor wages were the lucky ones because hordes of others had no work at all and existed off charity or from hand to mouth. We had seen the General Strike in 1926 when the country was brought to a standstill, but the ruling classes soon prevailed. There was still a 'them and us' division in the land. Britain had voted in a Labour government under J Ramsay MacDonald, but to no avail it seemed. Unemployment would continue to rise during the 1930s and fine words from speakers in city squares did little to change things.

Above: The war had been over for the best part of a year and these children were celebrating Empire Day in Heaton, to the northeast of the city centre. They waved their flags with gusto, but in truth the world had changed and the British Empire was in the early stages of coming apart. The glue that held it together had started to fail. Before long India, that jewel in the British crown, would be independent and the new country of Pakistan be formed. Elsewhere in the world, other nations across Asia and Africa started steps along the road to establishing their own identities, free from the yoke of British control. Empire Day was established in 1904 by Lord Meath. It was celebrated across the parts of the globe where the colour red predominated on maps. As the British Empire disintegrated, the day was rechristened Commonwealth Day in recognition of new relationships in post-colonial times.

Bottom left and below: You would have to travel a long way to see a better display of coronation decorations than these along Grey Street. The centrepiece of this photograph is the single-decker coronation bus with a similarly decorated double-decker version following close behind. They succeeded in turning heads wherever they went in the city. On the left the Royal Turk's Head had entered into the spirit of the occasion with an impressive display of its own. The property is no longer an hotel and was altered in 1991 along with some of the other properties on the block. In the distance, on the right, is the magnificent Theatre Royal. It dates from 1836 though it has been extensively restored on at least two occasions since then. It remains one of the most impressive buildings in Newcastle.

Below and inset: The Royal Agricultural Show was only held in Newcastle five times, and was to eventually find a permanent site in Warwickshire. It always attracted a huge number of visitors, and not just those interested in farming and agriculture! The Show, with its many fascinating displays to view, animals to interest the children, and bands to sit and listen to, made a great day out for the entire family. Preparations for the Show started well in advance of the big day as the stands were erected, displays set up, plant and machinery moved in, catering arranged, and a thousand and one other tasks dealt with. Visitors of quite a different kind opted to view the equestrian events, and our photograph would indicate that the Duke of Northumberland was a prizewinner in one of the

riding events. The Duke would soon find himself the fortunate possessor of the silver trophy, temptingly displayed on the table in the foreground of the picture, to be presented to him by the Queen Mother, who had a genuine interest in the riding events. There were no spare seats in the stand that day, and one or two people in the crowd have their cameras ready to record the prizegiving ceremony.

Above: Newcastle played host to the Royal Agricultural Show in 1956 before it eventually found a permanent home in the Midlands. In keeping with its title, notable visitors included the Duke of Northumberland and Queen Elizabeth, the late Queen Mother. This general view inside the grounds shows some of the trade stands with occupiers as diverse as Calor Gas and purveyors of sheep dips. Elsewhere, signs for bee-keeping demonstrations and flower displays capture the rural spirit of the occasion. Within the show there were parades of cattle and horseflesh, all competing to win rosettes within their respective categories. Large marquees offered the opportunity to view exhibitions of country crafts or the chance to sit down to a refreshing cup of tea. The whole environment hummed with activity and the strong animal aromas of the countryside. Riders demonstrated their equestrian skills in the show ring and sheepdogs were put through their paces to the accompaniment of piercing whistles and calls from their owners. Country squires rubbed shoulders with townies as the two life styles came together to enjoy the occasion that gave a flavour of the work of a sector of the community that still existed in our green and pleasant land. There were even prizes for displays of vegetables where allotment holders could compete with the most up to date of farmers. In the background fairground rides buzzed with the excited voices of young children having a whale of a time.

Below: It is early 1965, and the gold mounted clock on the premises of the Northern Goldsmiths significantly reads 11am. Solemn crowds wait along Pilgrim Street, Northumberland Street and around into Blackett Street to pay their last respects to Winston Churchill, who had died on 24 January. Churchill's funeral was the largest state funeral in world history up to that point in time, with representatives from 112 nations present. By decree of the Queen, his body lay in state in Westminster Hall for three days and a state funeral service was held at St Paul's Cathedral on 30 January, 1965. Many who were in the Newcastle crowd that day would have been thinking back to October 1951, when the great man visited the city. That was an election year, and Churchill was in Newcastle as part of the Conservative Party's campaign. Then, they had lined the route along Grainger Street that Churchill's gleaming Rolls Royce would take, craning their necks to catch a glimpse of the leader whose familiar fat cigar and walking stick had, since World War II, become a patriotic symbol. As we know, the Conservatives won, albeit by a narrow margin, and at the age of 76 Churchill once more became Britain's Prime Minister. Failing health forced him to step down in 1955, but he continued as a backbencher until 1964.

Right: Jumping Jack Flash!...its Mick and Bianca, seen here at their hotel in Newcastle in March 1971. Mick Jagger and the rest of the Rolling Stones were in town to perform a gig on what became known as their 'Farewell Tour of Great Britain'. The Stones had not staged a tour proper in their homeland since autumn 1966. Now they were going out after having announced on the day of their first show that they were becoming tax exiles and decamping to the South of France. The group started with concerts in northern England in Newcastle and Manchester, with the Newcastle City Hall, Northumberland Road, as the local venue. It's hard to believe with today's concert prices that you could get to see the 'Stones' and supporting band 'The Groundhogs', for just 75p per ticket. Jagger, Richards and Co were no strangers to the region having played Newcastle City Hall four times between 1964-66. This was an era when chart bands would embark on one seemingly endless concert tour. Jagger married Nicaraguan-born Bianca De Macias, on 12 May, 1971, in Saint-Tropez.

Right: Mayor Doris Starkey is dwarfed by heavyweight sportsmen Roger Uttley and Henry Cooper at the Whit weekend celebrations at Newcastle's Exhibition Park in 1978. Sir Henry Cooper OBE KSG was a heavyweight boxer known for the effectiveness of his left hook, "Enry's 'Ammer", and his knockdown of the young Muhammad Ali. Cooper held the British, Commonwealth and European heavyweight titles several times throughout his career, and unsuccessfully challenged Ali for the world heavyweight championship in 1966. He retired after his controversial loss against Joe Bugner in 1971, but the organisers of the Newcastle event asked him to put on his gloves again. A ring was set up in the park as part of the celebrations, and he graciously agreed to get into the ring against a young lad from a local boxing club. Councillor Doris Starkey continued to represent Elswick Ward until 1981.

Parker domnick hunter
Celebrating 50 Years of Filtration

domnick hunter Engineers Ltd was formed in November 1963 by Keith Domnick and George Hunter. The business started in Keith's garage before moving into premises in Washington, Tyne & Wear.

Today, the business has two major Divisions, domnick hunter Filtration & Separation Division, based at Team Valley, focusing on compressed air treatment and gas generation and domnick hunter Process Filtration Division, which supplies liquid treatment and gas filters to a wide range of industries.

In the early days of the business, their initial product was an autoclave filter used on hospital steam sterilisers, a filter which continues in production to the present day. An oil removal filter was developed next: the first major client for the oil removal filter being IMI Norgren.

A decision was taken in the early 1970s to try and penetrate export markets therefore, between 1970 and 1973 numerous overseas distributors were appointed to provide support to customers locally.

In 1971, Keith Domnick sold part of his shareholding to Walter Alexander Limited, a company based in Falkirk, Scotland. Two years later George Hunter decided that he would also leave the company and sold the majority of his shares to Walter Alexander Ltd too.

As a result of successes with autoclave filtration, new products were being added and developed around this time; Oil-X filters were designed to remove bulk oil, oil aerosol and particulate from compressed air streams.

From these early products, a world-leading range of compressed air filters was developed and domnick hunter soon grew to be number one in the compressed air treatment market.

Bio-X filters were also developed to sterilise compressed air used in the pharmaceutical and food industries. Filter elements were fitted into stainless steel housings which could be steam sterilised in-situ. This was the genesis for the later formation of domnick hunter's Process Filtration Division and deservedly, domnick hunter was awarded the Queen's Award to Industry for Technological Innovation for development of the microfibre coalescing filter.

In 1975, another Queen's Award to Industry for Export Achievement was awarded in recognition of the Group's success, with exports now accounting for 60% of their turnover.

In 1973, domnick hunter had by then outgrown its premises in Washington and with 33 employees, they moved to a converted factory and offices in Birtley, County Durham.

Domnick Hunter (Engineers) Ltd.
Washington Steel Works
Washington · Co. Durham · England
Telephone: Washington 2591

These premises are still in use today, although over the years have been extensively modified, not least by the addition of a 45,000 sq. ft. factory built in 1978 incorporating new technical offices, high quality clean-room standard laboratories for product testing, new product development and liquid filter production.

Top: Founders, Keith Domnick (left) and George Hunter. Below left: domnick hunter Oil-X filters. Centre: An early company sign with the first domnick hunter logo. Below: domnick hunter's 33 employees and products pictured in 1973.

Meanwhile, during the early 1970s, the level of export business had increased considerably, and so had the range of products. The products continued to be technically advanced and to lead the world in their particular field. Over the years patents were obtained in all major countries to protect these product lines.

Keith Domnick remained as Managing Director until 1978. However, that year he resigned and immigrated to the USA and on January 1st 1979, Brian Thompson took over as Managing Director. Not long afterwards domnick hunter GmbH was formed in Krefeld, Germany allowing the company to give even better dedicated support to local customers.

domnick hunter's Process Filtration Division was formed in 1981. This Division expanded domnick hunter beyond compressed air treatment and into liquid filtration applications, covering markets from industrial manufacturing to food and beverage and pharmaceuticals.

In less than twenty years domnick hunter had grown from having 2 employees to 160 and in 1984 the development of the company's first membrane manufacturing process began; the Asypor membrane would come to be used in a wide variety of liquid filtration applications and is still used today.

To support the growth of the Process Filtration Division, a whole range of specialists were now employed, from microbiologists to chemical engineers and polymer technologists. A new building was also erected for membrane production.

The PNEUDRI patented modular desiccant compressed air dryer range was introduced in 1985 as part of the MAXI range. It was the first modular dryer in the world. That same year domnick hunter became a wholly owned subsidiary of Walter Alexander Industries PLC.

The following year a new subsidiary company, Tanlea Engineering Ltd was set up to manufacture key components for domnick hunter. New offices and laboratories were completed together with renovation of the original offices at Birtley. Meanwhile, what was now the domnick hunter Group, was re-organised into two operating Divisions: an Industrial Division for all aspects of compressed air products and a Process Division for all aspects of air sterilisation and liquid filters.

domnick hunter

*Top left: Keith Domnick receives the first Queen's Award in 1975. **Left:** Brian Thompson who became Managing Director in 1979. **Bottom:** The domnick hunter premises of the 1970s. **Above:** One of the first orders for PNEUDRI for the Central Electricity Generating Board, pictured shortly before dispatch. **Above right:** The former company logo which was first registered in 1987.*

In 1987, another landmark was achieved as domnick hunter became Britain's first filter company to obtain registration ISO 9001 British Quality Standard.

The year was further marked by the new extension to domnick hunter's headquarters at Birtley, opened by His Royal Highness, The Duke of Edinburgh.

To cap the year, the company was awarded the Queen's Award to Industry for Export Achievement for the Group's continued high level of export sales and domnick hunter Fabrication opened in Jarrow to manufacture carbon steel and stainless steel housings.

The awards and accolades continued to flow when a British Design Council Award was won by domnick hunter for its PNEUDRI compressed air desiccant dryer range in 1988. A Queen's Award to Industry for Technological Achievement was granted in the following year for the PNEUDRI desiccant dryers.

The decade would end with domnick hunter Inc. being formed in Charlotte, North Carolina, USA; domnick hunter Fabrication Ltd obtaining TUV approval for the manufacture of fabricated vessels for the German market and a new purpose-built (35,000 sq. ft.) factory opening at Team Valley, Gateshead for the production of Industrial Division products.

The 1990s began with domnick hunter Nihon opening in Kobe, Japan. The PNEUDRI Generation II dryer being launched and in 1991 subsidiaries were formed in both Canada and Singapore. During this time the company's Fabrication business was moved from Jarrow to Boldon.

Top: The newly extended headquarters at Birtley in 1987.
Above left and inset: HRH The Duke of Edinburgh officially opens the new laboratories and office block, 1987. Inset shows Technical Director, Jeff Porter, explaining the operation of a flushing rig to HRH The Duke of Edinburgh.
Above right: Parker domnick hunter's Boldon premises.

Even more critically, a management buyout was completed.

Brian Thompson was appointed Executive Director in 1992 and yet another subsidiary was formed, this time in Spain. 1992 was also the year that the company name changed to domnick hunter Group Ltd.

domnick hunter marked 30 years in business in 1993, with guests from all over the world attending a celebration of their anniversary. The year would also be marked by the acquisition of Nitrox Ltd which provided an entry into the nitrogen gas generation market and also that same year, by the establishment of a Chinese subsidiary based in Beijing.

domnick hunter Group PLC was floated on the London Stock Exchange in 1994 and was subsequently voted Newcomer of the Year. The flotation price per share on the first day of trading was 200p, valuing the Group at over £65M.

domnick hunter France was now established, followed the next year by an Australian subsidiary.

The new Industrial headquarters in Team Valley Trading Estate, Gateshead, Tyne & Wear, was officially opened by HRH the Duke of Kent in 1995 extending the business to over 100,000 sq. ft., with state-of-the-art development laboratories, manufacturing areas, offices and conference facilities.

An Indonesian Associate company, P.T. domnick hunter Indonesia Ltd was formed in 1996 and in 1997 a

Gas Generation Division was formed and a new range of nitrogen gas generators and hydrogen generators were introduced.

International expansion continued with domnick hunter SweTec established as the Swedish distributor for Process products in the Nordic countries. Elsewhere ZANDER Aufbereitungstechnik GmbH was acquired leading to domnick hunter's Industrial Division and ZANDER integrating operations worldwide.

Xebec in Canada was acquired in 1998. That year also saw multiple awards being achieved; the Queen's Award to Industry for Export Achievement, as well as a prestigious Millennium Products Award for the MAXIGAS nitrogen generator range. MAXIGAS had earlier been selected by the Design Council for the Products of the Millennium Award, a new ED200 energy-saving condensate drain won first place in Plant Engineering magazine's 'Product of the Year' competition whilst TURBOSEP won best product in the separation section of Filtration & Separation Publication Annual Awards.

domnick hunter Hiross (Italy) joined the group in 1999 adding world class refrigerated compressed air dryers to the Industrial Division's product portfolio. This enabled a comprehensive compressed air treatment product range to be provided to customers globally, together with a range of water chillers.

Top and below: Views inside the new domnick hunter production plant at Birtley in the late 1980s which was described at the time as the most modern of its type in the world. Centre: Products from the 1980s which helped put domnick hunter at the forefront of filtration.

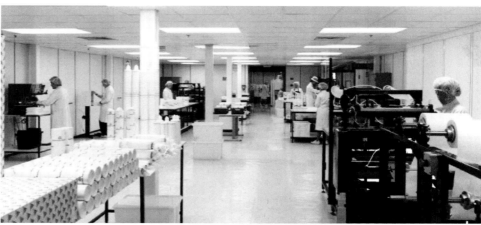

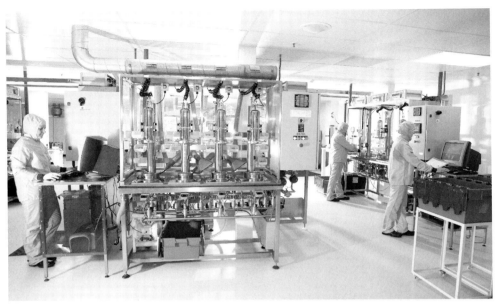

As new subsidiaries in Poland, the Czech Republic and India were formed, Process manufacturing doubled in size. By 2000 the Group turnover reached a record £103M.

In the opening year of the new millennium a brand-labelled supply agreement was concluded with Ingersoll Rand Inc. Elsewhere PNEUDRI MiDAS was launched and the Birtley site was now completely dedicated to Process Filtration operations, with substantial investment in clean room manufacturing facilities and laboratories.

domnick hunter Gas Generation Division won the Queen's Award for Enterprise for Innovation in 2002. A year later a manufacturing facility was established in China.

In 2004, the Process Division expanded globally through the acquisition of PTI Advanced Filtration Inc., based in Oxnard, California, and PTI Technologies Limited, based in Sheffield. The former provided the Division with its first manufacturing base in the United States. Meanwhile, the Process Division was not only awarded the Queen's Award for Enterprise within the International Trade category but also achieved ISO14001.

The following year, the next generation OIL-X filter & PNEUDRI dryer ranges and branded OIL-X EVOLUTION & PNEUDRI MX were launched for the compressed air treatment market.

2005 was also the year that domnick hunter was acquired by Parker Hannifin. Founded in 1918, the Parker story began when a 33-year-old engineer named Arthur Parker founded the Parker Appliance Company in Cleveland Ohio, to develop his unique braking system for trucks and buses.

With annual sales exceeding $13B in 2013, Parker Hannifin is the world's leading diversified manufacturer of motion and control technologies and systems providing precision-engineered solutions for a wide variety of mobile, industrial and aerospace markets. The company employs approximately 58,000 people in 50 countries around the world.

Parker's engineering expertise and broad range of core technologies uniquely positions the company to solve some of the world's greatest engineering challenges. By partnering with customers, Parker improves their productivity and profitability and seeks new ways to solve humanity's biggest challenges.

Parker can be found on and around everything that moves. It manufactures highly engineered components and systems that facilitate motion and the controlled flow of liquids and gases for a wide variety of global markets from aircraft and building infrastructure, to developing more efficient energy, advanced medical science and engineered materials, providing clean food and water, and supporting military efforts: Parker's thousands of employees work with customers to help solve the engineering challenges they encounter all across the globe.

Despite the change of ownership in 2008 Parker domnick hunter's progress continued with their membrane factory in Etten Leur, in the Netherlands, achieving AS9100 Aerospace accreditation.

Top left: A view inside the Parker domnick hunter state-of-the-art production plant, 2013. Left: A selection of the Parker domnick hunter filters and small dryers. Above: Parker domnick hunter logo after the Parker acquisition.

Two years later the company gained its ninth Queen's Award for Enterprise (International Trade) given to Parker domnick hunter Filtration & Separation Division for its MAXIGAS Nitrogen product.

domnick hunter Industrial Division changed its name to domnick hunter Filtration and Separation Division in 2011 and the Process Division won UK Factory of the Year run by Cranfield University School of Management and Works Management. The Process Division also expanded its product range for the emerging biopharmaceutical market with the integration of Mitos in Phoenixville, Pennsylvania, North America. Mitos provides them with disposable bags, tubing and connectors for biopharmaceutical manufacturing.

Meanwhile, a global laboratory network was being developed to support Process Filtration business growth and at home, the domnick hunter Filtration and Separation Division won the North East Chamber of Commerce Export Team Award. Elsewhere, the new Nitrogen SmartFluxx Nitrogen Membrane was launched.

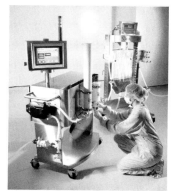

Parker domnick hunter Process Division continued its expansion by acquiring SciLog Inc. in Madison, Wisconsin, in 2012 adding the manufacture of sensor technology and laboratory systems for the biopharmaceutical industry to the Group.

Twin Filter BV was then acquired by the Process Division, developing a leading market position in filtration applications for the oil and gas industry.

From its small beginnings in 1963, Parker domnick hunter now has more than 1000 employees worldwide, a turnover in excess of $500M and is represented in 50 countries.

Fifty years of remarkable progress and here's to the next fifty years!

Top left: The Group receives its ninth Queen's Award - the Queen's Award for Enterprise, 2010. Left: The domnick hunter Process Division was proud to receive UK Factory of the Year Award in 2011. Below left: The Parker domnick hunter Process Division in Birtley, County Durham. Top right: At work in SciLog Inc., Madison, Wisconsin. Above: Twin Filter BV products. Below: Parker domnick hunter's Filtration and Separation Division in Team Valley Trading Estate, Gateshead.

STREET SCENES

Above: In 1935 Northumberland Street was offering its loyal greetings to King George V on the occasion of his silver jubilee, having acceded to the throne on the death of his father, Edward VII on 6 May 1910. George V was a popular monarch who pleased the public when he renounced his family's Germanic name of Saxe-Coburg-Gotha in 1917, replacing it with Windsor. He was also appreciated for his dislike of most things foreign, saying, 'Abroad? Been there once; didn't like it.' The public was glad to celebrate his 25 years on the throne as it had little other reason to party during those days of depression and high unemployment. We can see how busy Northumberland Street had become even all that long time ago, with cars and trams clogging the road making life difficult for pedestrians. In later years a footbridge was built over the end of Northumberland Street, near to Burton's, the site of the present Monument Mall. To the right was the Queen's Hall, originally intended to be a 2,500-seater concert hall, hotel and 1,000 seat cinema when plans were unveiled in 1911. This ambitious project was shelved and the smaller cinema built in 1913. On this day, Cicely Courtneidge (1893-1980) was starring in the movie 'Things are Looking Up', an optimistic title in those days for a film that told of a circus horsewoman who has to pose as her schoolmistress sister. Born in Sydney, she played musical comedy and revue, both in a celebrated partnership with her husband, Jack Hulbert, and as a highly talented comedienne in her own right. She became a Dame in 1972.

Right: A photograph dating from May 1953 and showing that the decorations for the coronation of the new Queen were already beginning to brighten up the centre of Newcastle. The location is Market Street and it can be seen that the major stores, including Binns and Bainbridge's were taking the event very seriously. Back in the day Binns and Bainbridge's department stores were two of the best-loved shops in Newcastle. Both stores date back to the 19th century and in 1849, Bainbridge's became the first department store in the world. Who can forget seeing the slogan 'Shop at Binns' on the front of every Northern bus.

Above: Part of the city wall in the Bath Lane area of Newcastle, with the neatly laid out paved area, raised flower beds and wooden benches, had been recently renovated when this scene was captured in March 1961. Referred to as 'an oasis within the city' by the planners it was intended as an area of rest and relaxation for tired shoppers and passers-by. The Essoldo cinema can just be seen at the top of the photograph. It opened in 1938, the first feature being The Hurricane starring Dorothy Lamour. The Essoldo had the distinction of being the first cinema in Newcastle to show the block-busting movie Gone with the Wind. The cinema changed name many times, particularly in the last few years of its operation. It finally closed in January 1990, the last film shown there being Shirley Valentine. The building was pulled down in 1991.

Above: This is a great photograph with a feeling of period atmosphere, taken in 1956. Pedestrians take their life in their hands as they cross the busy road at Marlborough Crescent, long before the days when white zig-zags warned of the approach to a crossing. The ladies in the picture may have been en-route to the shops and all are well wrapped up against the cold weather of late October. Marlborough Crescent was ringed with small shops ...probably newsagents, cafés, confectioners and tobacconists... all subsisting on trade from the bus station. Marlborough Bus Station was erected during the 1920s, and was eventually closed and levelled to be used as a car park. A building contractor used the office building for many years before it was reclaimed and restored during the building of the International Centre for Life visitor attraction.

Below: Still easily recognisable as the Collingwood Street, Westgate Road and Neville Street area of the city to modern residents despite there having been some major construction work here since this picture was taken in 1959. The buildings on the left of the picture, including the old offices of the Newcastle Chronicle and Journal and Norwich Union, have been pulled down to make way for a huge office block. Most of the buildings that remain have, at some time, had the bulk of the black soot removed from their exterior, giving the streets along here a much brighter appearance. The five storey building housing Barclays Bank was notable for the magnificent plasterwork on the ground floor banking hall. The building was opened in 1905.

Above: George Binns founded a modest drapery business on High Street, Sunderland, in 1807, but it is the department stores in many towns and cities, inspired by his grandson J J Binns, that we all remember with great affection. By the early days of the 20th century the chain's array of London and Paris fashions and elegant costumes had attracted such a reputation for excellence that the business became like Topsy as it just 'growed and growed'. The Newcastle store stood on the corner of Market Street and Grey Street. Although gobbled up by the House of Fraser in the 1950s, it continued to trade under its original name in order to preserve traditional customer links. The store occupied the building now known as Earl Grey House, where Costa Coffee came to be situated in more recent times.

Right: Fenwick's department store was one of those long established shops that had its own particular clientele who found it to be a tried and trusted outlet. Opening on Northumberland Street in 1882, it is still trading today having served umpteen generations of customers. Everyone looks forward to the store's Christmas window display, always one of the retail highlights of the season.

Great grandmas bring their little ones to see the grand old white bearded man in a red suit, just as they had been brought along themselves so many years before. The window display here dates from 1958 and is a much more summery scene, with its show of 'out and about' separates. Fenwick's has become one of Britain's largest luxury stores.

Above: This breathtaking picture was taken from Grey's monument and shows the handsome sweep of Grey Street, giving a glorious view of the stunning architecture that is the pride of Newcastle. Its beauty and grandeur are acknowledged worldwide, and, from the evidence of the photograph taken in 1957, it is not hard to see the reason why. Lloyd's Bank, formerly the Northumberland and District Bank, the building in the foreground, has corner bays that were once private houses used by bank officials, tellers and clerks. The building's exterior was renovated in the 1980s and the interior remodelled. To the left of centre we can see the Theatre Royal. The first building to have this name was designed by David Stephenson and erected in 1788 on Mosley Street, whereas our present theatre dates from just before Queen Victoria came to the throne. Constructed by John and Benjamin Green, the Theatre Royal opened on 20 February, 1837, with a production of 'The Merchant of Venice'. Perhaps someone mentioned the name 'Macbeth' in 1899 because misfortune struck the theatre when it was badly damaged by fire following a performance of 'the Scottish play'. It reopened in 1901 and, apart from a two-year closure for restoration in 1986, has continued to present a cultural face to the world, in keeping with the majesty of Grey Street.

Below It was April 1968, and the lack of buses gives us a hint that a total of 1,400 corporation bus drivers were on strike at the time. Blackett Street was empty of all but private cars, and there are remarkably few of them about in this interesting shot. The umbrellas, puddles and windscreen wipers tell us that this was hardly the best date that could have been chosen for a bus strike; the end of the day would see a host of tired and dejected workers making their way home with sore feet and shortened tempers. This scene has changed almost beyond recognition today. The rather nice YMCA building was built in 1896, and is typical of the ornate and solidly respectable Victorian architecture that was common at the time. This is the focal point of the City Centre area is Grey's Monument located at the top end of Grey Street, regarded by some as one of the finest streets in the country. The Monument Metro Station, Eldon Square and Monument Mall shopping centres are all situated around this area.

Right: Northumberland Street has always had an overwhelming choice of stores since it was established as a major shopping street at the end of the 19th century. Accustomed as we are to seeing this part of Northumberland Street as a traffic free zone, it seems rather strange to look back to the days when buses and cars were seen here. This view dates from October 1986, and the pavements were crowded in this shoppers' paradise. The flagship stores of Marks & Spencer, Woolworths, Fenwicks and Littlewoods - all invited passers-by to part with their cash. John J Fenwick's first shop, pictured in the foreground on the left, was originally at No5 Northumberland Street, where, pandering to the fashion of the day, they sold mantles and furs. This was in the days before the tide of public opinion swung violently against the wearing of animal fur.

The Bigg Market, whose name refers to barley rather than size (which they say doesn't matter), is nevertheless a little gem. It is the city's oldest market and dates back to Norman times. This fantastic pigeon's eye view of the market and surrounding area gives us a wider perspective, and captures the old Town Hall before it was demolished and replaced by a modern office block. It will undoubtedly revive many memories for readers of a certain age. We can make a guess at the time of year looking at the banner for the Tyneside Summer Exhibition, which was a permanent feature of the Newcastle summer and held at Exibition Park. Taken in the mid-60s, we can also clearly see the Rutherford Memorial and the historic underground toilets directly behind it. The subterranean loos have been a city centre fixture for those wanting to spend a penny, for more than a century. Dr John Hunter Rutherford (1826-1890) was an evangelist and preacher from Jedburgh who had a church in Bath Lane.

This view from Byker, taken in 1974, shows a panorama of the city in the distance. The camera was pointed west, looking down along Conyers Road. Over to the left we can see the rear of the old Shipley Street Baths.

Near there now is Byker Wall, a block of 620 maisonettes that was erected in the 1970s. The A193 bypass has replaced the pavement to the right and a cycle path and walkway have been created across the centre where the railway fencing used to be.

Most of the area in the foreground was razed and redeveloped. In the distance are the towers of St Nicholas Cathedral, All Saints' Church and St Ann's Church, standing aloof above the mess below.

Above: Well, if we cannot get to the sands on Whitley Bay, then they will have to come to us. These enterprising children were making sand pies and castles out of the mud and debris left behind by demolition workers. The land around them had been cleared and soon the other houses nearby would be gone as well. Byker was scheduled for redevelopment in the 1970s. Much of the housing stock could be dated back to Victorian times and many homes were still without proper bathrooms. The Council had a policy of clearing the slums, but retaining the community. In 1969 Ralph Erskine was appointed as architect for the new Byker. The development was planned as a rolling programme so that residents remained in the area as building work took place in stages around them.

BUILDINGS, MONUMENTS & BRIDGES

Right: It is remarkable that John Dobson's House, New Bridge Street, was used as a glorified advertising site. The architect's home had been given little respect, becoming a mere billboard. Material displayed on such places has not changed much over time. This collection dates from 1911 but, in many respects, could apply to today's marketing strategies. Some of the products, names and content are not relevant now, but the idea of big, bold, eye-catching material is still important in the 21st century. There are some goods and services that mean little to young modern eyes, such as Virol, a malt extract given to children, or Kompo, a herbal concentrate to which water was added to make a drink. Some are self-explanatory and say all in the product name, as with Bournville cocoa, Robin starch or Globe metal polish. We can also make out an advert for the Tyne Theatre and Opera House that opened in 1867. This building later became a cinema before closing in 1974. Having been taken over by a charity, it reopened as a theatre in 1977. It continues to flourish today as the Mill Volvo Tyne Theatre.

Bottom left: The Exchange and Guild-Hall on the 'Sandhill' is the ancient centre of municipal government of the town. There is reference to the existence of a guildhall as early as 1400. In the 16th century, Newcastle had become one of England's most prosperous towns, with burgeoning textile and coalmining industries, and easy access to imported goods via the Tyne. The building was essentially the centre of the town's financial district, turning its back to the river at the east end of Sandhill. The old Exchange was rebuilt and enlarged in the middle of the 17th century by York architect, Robert Trollop, and most of the interior of the present building dates from 1658. The semicircle of columns on its east side was built to support a portico giving shelter to a fish market. Newcastle's famous 19th century architect, John Dobson, designed them. This photograph dates from 1928. This was a historical year for women in then UK when The Representation of the People (Equal Franchise) Act 1928 extended the voting franchise to all women over the age of 21, granting women the vote on the same terms as men.

Left: The photographer of this aerial view is to be congratulated in bringing this stunning view to us. Captured in 1950, the shutter clicked to take in the Haymarket, St Thomas' Church, the bus stands and the war memorial. Even now, despite the enclosure of the bus station and the looming presence of the 1968 civic centre behind the church, this is an instantly recognisable part of the city. Looking roughly northeast from above Percy Street, 'Winged Victory', the war memorial, rises in the centre of the image as a 70 feet high tapered, octagonal column that is a tribute to those who fell in the South African campaign or Boer War. It was during that conflict that the phrase 'concentration camp' came into being - a term with even more horrific connotations during World War II. St Thomas' Church, built in 1850, stands somewhat confusingly on St Mary's Place. This address was taken from the former medieval leper hospital, St Mary Magdalene, that once stood near here. In modern times, the road leading left from the memorial goes to Barras Bridge before heading off to a junction with the A167M from where it becomes the Great North Road to Gosforth and beyond.

Below: This general view of Newcastle Quayside was taken from across the water above Gateshead in 1950. Among many other notable buildings, the 1929 Salvation Army Men's Palace can be seen next to All Saints' Church. This place of worship, designed by David Stephenson, replaced All Hallows in 1780. Unusual in its oval shape, the church was deconsecrated in 1961, a comment on the decline in fortunes of this part of Newcastle in those days. The building was converted into offices in 1984 and partly used as a school resource centre. The Quayside is the oldest part of the city and was once the keystone of its commercial activity. Until major 19th century building works got under way, the castle keep and the 14th century St Nicholas' Church, and from 1882 the cathedral, with its distinctive lantern tower, were the major landmarks in the area. In more modern times, regeneration along here has returned the Quayside to a position as one of the focal points of Newcastle activity. Bars, clubs, theatres and cosmopolitan restaurants have revitalised it into a buzzing centre once more.

Right: A contrast between the old and the new is evident in this picture from 1957. The location of the scene is the junction of Benton Road and the Coast Road. The modern shopping development on the right looks out across the broad, shallow roundabout where a gardener can be seen leaning on his rake and admiring his work. Overhead, the wires for the trolley bus service are visible, supported by the long crooked poles as they hum with the current necessary to power the vehicles. Notice the motorcycle combination approaching the roundabout. The mature rider isn't wearing a helmet - it wasn't a legal requirement in those days.

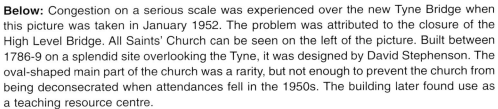

Below: Congestion on a serious scale was experienced over the new Tyne Bridge when this picture was taken in January 1952. The problem was attributed to the closure of the High Level Bridge. All Saints' Church can be seen on the left of the picture. Built between 1786-9 on a splendid site overlooking the Tyne, it was designed by David Stephenson. The oval-shaped main part of the church was a rarity, but not enough to prevent the church from being deconsecrated when attendances fell in the 1950s. The building later found use as a teaching resource centre.

Left: Here we have a dramatic bird's eye view of the part of the city centre that includes Percy Street, Newgate Street, St Andrew's Church and Eldon Square as it all looked in 1950. We can tell from this photograph that Newcastle was fortunate in comparison with some other major cities. Most of our historic buildings survived and we were spared the excesses of modern architecture inflicted upon our urban cousins elsewhere in the country. St Andrew's, perhaps our oldest church, was spared, along with Eldon Square, at the bottom left of the picture. In 1950, trees and pleasant architecture flanked this green oasis. Compare it now with the scene we have in the 21st century as the Eldon Square shopping centre dominates the bottom part of this scene. It hovers over the roadway and throws its shadows across the statue of St George, like some sort of Martian war machine from a story by H G Wells.

Right: St George has been slaying the dragon in Eldon Square for longer than he cares to remember. It is we who are the ones who need to recall what he stands for as C I Hartwell designed the bronze statue as a memorial to those who fell in the two world wars. St George, the patron saint of the Northumberland Fusiliers, sits in the square completed by Grainger in 1826. It was named for one of the Royal Grammar School's famous old boys, John Scott, Earl of Eldon and Lord High Chancellor of England for most of the period 1801-27. He resigned his post in protest against the Catholic Emancipation plan of the prime minister, George Canning. Nor would he have slept easy when the backdrop to this 1956 scene was replaced by the institutional facade of the Eldon Shopping Centre. In the 1960s the west and north terraces around the square were demolished to be replaced by part of the Shopping Centre, which now dominates Old Eldon Square. Some renovation was completed in 2008 and the square now features new landscaping and ground level access to the shopping centre. Still today, the square attracts people to sit on the benches and the grass in the summer sun.

Right: The main building of the Newcastle Royal Victoria Infirmary can be seen here in this photograph from 1964. It was opened in 1906 by King Edward VII and replaced the original Infirmary that had existed on the Forth Banks site since 1753. Donations from the Hall and Armstrong families totalling over £200,000 had made the construction of the new building possible. The fully furnished and equipped hospital, containing twenty wards, a nurses' home, chapel and five operating theatres, cost over £300,000. The statue of Queen Victoria was the gift of Riley Lord, who was knighted for his efforts in getting the Infirmary built. The 1960s were a decade of change. Gone were the grey, austere days of the 50s. The 60s were chic, sharp and cool and some of the cars that came from those golden years were legendary, whilst others should, perhaps, be quietly forgotten. Some of the best examples can be seen in the Infirmary car park including, Morris Minor, Ford Cortina Mk1, Rover P6, MGB, Mini and a Jaguar Mark 2.

'I'll meet you under the clock.' How often has this phrase been uttered by travellers down the years since the Central Station was first opened? The lakes of water on the concourse tell us that the clock had obviously had a narrow escape when these scenes were captured back in July 1961. The wooden cladding on John Dobson's magnificent vaulted ceiling has clearly been under threat; high pressure jets of water play on the roof as fire crews battle to save this important part of Newcastle's history, while water still cascades down from the roof in our dramatic photograph.

The smoke charred walls and piles of rubble and debris within the station concourse tell us that it was a near thing, and crowds of would-be passengers gather together out of harm's way. This was not the first time fire had threatened the station, and nor would it be the last, the latest having been as recent as 1997. The Central Station is a marvel of Victorian engineering, combining artistic and graceful lines with practical use. Queen Victoria and Prince Albert visited Newcastle to declare the station - built at a cost of £100,000 - officially open on 29 August, 1850.

Above: Newcastle upon Tyne, and the area surrounding it, is famous for its bridges across the River Tyne. The bridges seem to define what Newcastle was, and is, about. A great engineering heritage and a forward-looking modern city and great sights when 'walking the quays', mainly on the Newcastle side of the River Tyne. The four bridges seen in this photograph from 1930 are: the Tyne Bridge (road), the road Swing Bridge, the High Level Bridge and the Queen Elizabeth II Bridge. The latter carries the Tyne and Wear Metro railway line from Gateshead, across the River Tyne to Newcastle city centre.

Right: The story of Newcastle's Swing Bridge takes us back to the mid 19th century, and the days when a Georgian stone bridge crossed the Tyne at this point. Seagoing vessels, of course, could go no further than the bridge, which did not matter too much until W G Armstrong's Elswick Works began to expand and develop. The engineering firm originally built hydraulic machines, but as the company extended their operations into shipbuilding and armaments the stone bridge presented a real problem. The new double cantilevered 1,200 ton Swing Bridge was designed and paid for by Armstrong, with work beginning

in 1873. It was first used for road traffic on 15 June, 1876, and opened for river traffic a month later. Originally driven by steam (though replaced by electric pumps in 1959), the hydraulic machinery pivoted the bridge through 180 degrees to allow for the passage of ships. At its peak in 1924 the bridge could swing up to 6,000 times in the year. By the 1970s this had dropped to around 900, with each swing taking six minutes.

The Tyne Bridge is one of Newcastle's most famous icons and a symbol of Tyneside's industrial pride. Construction of the bridge was still in progress when this magnificent view was captured for posterity. Designed by the engineering firm Mott, Hay and Anderson, work started in August 1925 with Dorman Long of Middlesbrough acting as the building contractors. Men risked their lives high above the waters of the Tyne, scaling heights and structures with the agility of Spiderman. The arch of the bridge curves elegantly away from us - at the time a great design coup for the city, as the Tyne Bridge had the largest arch anywhere in Britain. In their admiration of the bridge itself, many fail to appreciate the pairs of Cornish granite towers that support the bridge at each end. Designed by the well-known Newcastle architect Robert Burns Dick, the impressive twin towers remind one of the medieval castles of long ago. The opening of the bridge by King George V and the Queen who were the first to use the roadway in 1928 was a red letter day in Newcastle, and there was a holiday atmosphere among the motorists who came from far and wide to cross the bridge. To the dismay of some locals, several pubs had to be demolished to make way for the bridge - they included the Goat Inn, the Earl of Durham, the Ridley Arms and the Steamboat Inn.

NEWCASTLE UNITED F.C.

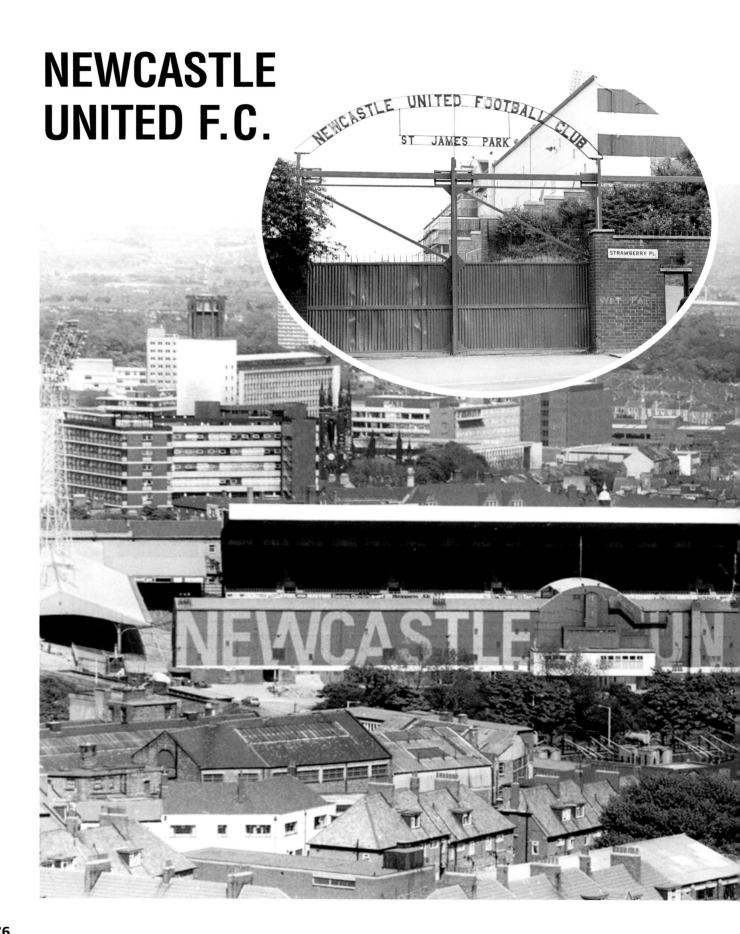

Top left and left: To a Magpie fan this is the best photograph in the world: St James' Park in all its glory. The oldest football stadium in the North East has been the home ground of Newcastle United since 1892 and has been used for football since 1880. The stadium was first used by United after the unification of Newcastle East End and Newcastle West End. Back in Victorian Tyneside, St James Park was barely a rough patch of grazing land, situated on a small hill overlooking the city and part of the historic Town Moor. It had a notorious slope, a drop of fully 18 feet from the north to south goal. Local butchers could still graze their animals on the pitch before being led to slaughter. While the stadium is now synonymous with the 'Black and Whites', Newcastle United actually played in red and white at St James' Park until 1904. In 1905, a doubling of capacity to 60,000, with a main stand on the Barrack Road (now Milburn Stand), and major other stands, produced a state-of-the-art facility.

Above: At the Newcastle v Sunderland derby at St. James Park in 1904, Lord Beresford, Admiral of the Channel Fleet, is about to kick off the match. Rivalries make the footballing world go round the globe, but in Britain, few retain the kind of intensity served up by supporters of Newcastle United and Sunderland. The first meeting between the two took place in 1883, with the first competitive fixture an FA Cup tie in 1888. Lord Charles Beresford was a British admiral and Member of Parliament between 1859 and 1916. He combined the two careers of the navy and MP, gaining a reputation as a hero in battle and champion of the navy in the House of Commons. He was a well-known and popular figure who courted publicity, widely known to the British public as "Charlie B". He was considered by many to be a personification of John Bull, and indeed was normally accompanied by his trademark, a bulldog. Newcastle United won the Football League championship in the 1904-05 season. The club also reached the FA Cup Final that year but was beaten by Aston Villa 2-0. The attendance of 101,117 remains the largest crowd to watch Newcastle play.

During the 1950s United lifted the FA Cup on three occasions within a magic five year period. In 1951 they defeated Blackpool 2-0, a year later and Arsenal were dispatched 1-0 and in 1955, United cruised past Manchester City by a 3-1 scoreline. This was the great era of John Edward Thompson and 'Wor Jackie' Milburn, who contributed significantly to Newcastle United's

unparalleled success. Team manager during the 1951 and 1952 FA Cup Final wins was Stan Seymour, who was in his second spell at the club, having been manager from 1939 to 1947 as well. Stan Seymour (pictured top right) was a footballer who played, managed, was chairman and a director of Newcastle United. Born in Kelloe, Seymour is one of the all-time Newcastle United greats, and was known

as 'Mr. Newcastle United' after the various years and roles he delivered for the club. Thousands line the streets of Newcastle to welcome home the victorious FA Cup winning team from 1952. Magpie fans cheered and waved as their heroes passed in open topped coaches. The FA Cup is clearly in view and the players took it in turns to hold the trophy aloft. Fans of all ages and sexes had turned out to pay homage to their idols. As the coaches travelled along Westgate Road, people in the office buildings along the roadside can be seen precariously hanging out of upper windows to get a better view. This was all made possible after Chilean George Robledo had scored the only goal in the 1952 Final, in a tough game at Wembley. Back-to-back FA Cup wins led to them becoming known locally as 'the team of the century'.

Below, right and top right: The Fifties were a golden age for football with crowds flocking to games at every level. The big city clubs began to dominate the FA Cup, with Newcastle regarding Wembley as their second home. The great era of 'Wor' Jackie Milburn brought Newcastle United unparalleled success. Jackie was blisteringly quick, a former Powderhall sprinter. No other United player scored more goals in all competitions for the Magpies, while he also scored in every round of the 1951 FA Cup Final run. As the previous pages show, Geordie fans turned out in force to celebrate as Newcastle won the FA Cup on consecutive seasons in 1951/2, beating first Blackpool and then Arsenal at Wembley a year later. Excited fans lined the streets as the triumphant cavalcade, carrying their heroes, travelled along Westgate Road past the Norwich Union Insurance offices. It seemed like most of Newcastle had turned out to pay homage to their favourite team and 'welcome hyem the canny lads', which included the likes of Len Shackleton, Jackie Milburn, Bobby Mitchell and Jack Fairbrother.

Right: The historic goal-scoring duo of John Tudor and Malcom 'Supermac' Macdonald are seen here in action in a game from the 1972-73 season. They both signed for Newcastle in 1971 and developed a prolific partnership, helping the "Toon" win the Anglo-Italian Cup, and two Texaco Cup's in the mid-70s. Supermac was a fans favourite, built like a middle-weight boxer. He was a brash and colourful centre-forward who lived for hitting the ball into the back of the net. Tudor, on the other hand, was more of a willing workhorse who would chase lost causes, which made him the ideal strike partner.

GETTING AROUND

Above: They look more like Airfix kits than fully fledged flying machines, but these are the sorts of pioneering craft that took the Wright brothers aloft, Blériot over the Channel and saw Tommy Sopwith found a School of Aviation. The planes were on Gosforth Park as part of a competition that began at Brooklands in Surrey in July 1911 and, with stops at various control points such as Harrogate and Newcastle, they went to Edinburgh and Stirling before heading back south to Brighton. There was prize money of £10,000 awarded by the Daily Mail for the quickest pilot over the 1,000-mile journey. The race took a fortnight to complete and was won by a French Navy officer, Lt JL Conneau under the pseudonym André Beaumont, flying a Blériot XI.

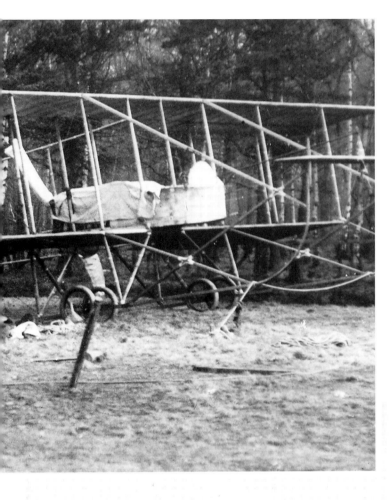

Bottom left: Captain Dawes, on the right, was in his flying garb at Gosforth Park, having completed one of many legs of the 1911 Circuit of Britain competition. He was chatting to two other Army officers, Captain Longcroft and Lieutenant Herbert. There was no such service as the RAF in those days, with its forerunner the Royal Flying Corps not coming into being until 1912. Even then it was regarded as a branch of the Army, rather having a separated identity.

Below: The crowds at Gosforth Park marvelled at the sight of such magnificent flying machines. It was less than a decade since Orville and Wilbur Wright demonstrated their invention that managed a brief hop over a matter of yards and established them as pioneers of powered flight. Now here we were, watching a race up and down Britain that had stages totalling some 1,000 miles with individual legs of anything from 20 to 150 miles at a time. French aviators took first and second place in the competition, with the British flag being flown by James Valentine in third place. He was killed in 1917 on active duty near Kiev as a Lieutenant Colonel in the Royal Flying Corps.

Below: The rolling stock stood idle. The carriages belonging to the North Eastern Railway were not going anywhere. This was the scene during the first ever national strike to be called on the railways. It was born of a long-standing dispute between workers and the rail companies' owners, along with the desire of the trades unions to flex their muscles. A series of unofficial strikes took place in the summer of 1911, leading to this national show of unity that lasted for two days. Prime Minister Asquith and Home Secretary Churchill gave permission for police and troops to be used to keep the locomotives moving. This action led to the Llanelli Riots in which six workers were killed.

Left: During the rail strike of 1911, people sat around on station platforms waiting for the troops to get the trains moving as the workers spent 48 hours manning picket lines and holding rallies that demanded better negotiating procedures with the employers over pay and conditions. These were early days for concerted and organised industrial action by trade union members. This conflict produced some positive results in that the Liberal government of the day was forced to set up a Royal Commission to examine the workings of the 1907 Conciliation Board.

Bottom right: No this is not what happens to passengers if they wait around for trains that don't arrive on time, and British Rail have not been reduced to running on a skeleton staff. This skeleton was discovered in a large black trunk in a storage room at Manors Station, Newcastle on 5 February, 1976. Manors railway station is on the East Coast Main Line. It was previously a much larger and more significant station at the junction of the East Coast Main Line and the line towards Gosforth. Most of the station was closed in 1978 when the Gosforth line was turned over to the Tyne and Wear Metro and the buildings were subsequently demolished to make way for offices. Manors station opened on 30 August, 1850, to replace a temporary station that became a coal depot, and had two platforms on a bridge over Trafalgar Street. The station is very popular with railway photographers and trainspotters because it lies in the middle of the tracks of the East Coast Main Line allowing very good views of passing trains, which include freight, passenger and empty stock movements.

Above: Things have not changed much since 1924. Road repairing still needs at least one man to lean on a shovel, several more to stand around and one worker to drive the machinery. New roads were being built to cater for the rapidly increasing demands of both public and private motor vehicles. The number of these on our thoroughfares rose dramatically after the Great War and at least it was one growth industry in a world that was lurching towards a major recession.

Right: The junction of Lisle Street and Northumberland Street is now part of the paved, pedestrianised section of the central city shopping area. Back in 1955, it was part of the normal thoroughfare and needed to be kept open for traffic, as far as was humanly possible. Snow is a lovely white, delicate and powdery delight. Well, it is on Christmas cards and in the movies. In real life, it soon turns to mucky, slushy stuff that makes you wet, cold and generally frustrated trying to make a way through it, whether on foot or by car.

Right: Under the present system, a vehicle with a registration mark beginning FT would be from the Fens in Lincolnshire. But, earlier plates with this pair of letters indicated one from Newcastle-upon-Tyne. It was on 1 January, 1904, that it became compulsory to sport such means of identification. The highly prized A1 was allocated to Earl Russell. Initially, details of cars and motorcycles were kept in separate registers, so it was possible for two vehicles to be given the same alphanumeric plate. Pictured in 1908, this bright and breezy couple in their motor cycle and basket style sidecar was part of the vanguard of early motorists. The twosome must have been keen as this form of transport was not for the fainthearted in the north east's nippy weather. Note the period acetylene powered lamps and slim tyres.

Left: Motorists who are used to driving in today's hectic traffic conditions often look back with nostalgia to the 'good old days' of the 1950s and 60s when there was comparatively little traffic on the roads. It takes photographs such as this one to demonstrate just how short our memories are! It was the build up of vehicles in the city centre and the resulting congestion that called for the urgent action that led to the sweeping changes of the mid 1960s. John Dobson Street was laid out, alleviating the demands on Northumberland Street; the new Central Motorway cut a swathe through the city, and the Pilgrim Street Roundabout swept away many old and familiar buildings. Our photograph is dated 19 September, 1961, and the view captured looking north along Pilgrim Street would within a few short years change out of all

recognition. The Royal Arcade on the right was one of the many casualties of progress. The scene brings back memories of the lorries that were typical of the day and the vehicles we once drove. The family saloon in the foreground looks like a Vauxhall Victor and the original Victor became Britain's most exported car. On the corner of Moseley Street we can see Van der Velde office equipment, established in Newcastle since 1862, Van der Velde has a history in the service business from the early days of typewriters all the way to state of the art networking today.

Below: Patient resignation is on the face of each of these would-be passengers queuing hopefully for their bus at the end of yet another working day. A hot meal will be waiting for some of them, and after that they could look forward to a couple of hours with their mates in the 'Dog and Duck'. If they were the type to enjoy the fireside rather than the tap room, it would be pipe and slippers time, with 'Crossroads', 'Take Your Pick' or perhaps 'Emergency Ward Ten' to watch on TV. This busy shot of the Worswick Street Bus Station is dated October 1962, the days when feminists had only just begun to burn their bras, and there were still a large number of women who counted themselves as housewives. Their job was shopping, bringing up the children, cleaning the house, and making sure their man - who was the breadwinner - had a good meal every day. Scenes such as this were an everyday sight at Worswick Street; at the time around 150 buses left the bus station every hour.

Left: The open aspect of the forecourt and the garb of the men at the pumps might make a reader think of Route 66 or some other American highway. Nothing so fancy, for this was the face of Benton Oval service station on 2 August, 1962. The various cans were all made to exact specifications of volume and capacity and were being filled by the men from the weights and measures inspectorate. It was their job to check that retailers were not fiddling their customers and, having finished here, were off to check on the optics and pint pots of some poor landlord or the scales used by an unsuspecting grocer unaware of their imminent arrival. Usually the general public is suspicious and aggressive towards certain types of officialdom, but these men were on our side and if they could squeeze an extra drop of fuel from those pumps for our tanks, so much the better. The self-service petrol station was becoming more common in the early 1960s. Where once an attendant leapt from his kiosk, checked oil and water levels, wiped the windscreen and then dispensed the petrol for us there was now no one in sight. We were left to do the lot for ourselves in the name of progress.

Newcastle Central is one of the great monuments of the early Railway Age. It is also remains an important and busy station, despite the loss of much of its suburban traffic to the Tyne & Wear Metro. The station was designed by the architect John Dobson and built at the joint expense of the Newcastle & Carlisle Railway (N&C) and George Hudson's Newcastle & Darlington Junction and Newcastle & Berwick Railways.

The station was constructed in collaboration with Robert Stephenson (also responsible for the High Level Bridge) between 1845 and 1850. The opening ceremony, attended by Queen Victoria, took place on 29 August 1850. The portico with which we are so familiar is a later edition to the station in 1863. Originally named Newcastle-on-Tyne Central, the station name was simplified to Newcastle at some point between 1948 and 1953.

Essentially, Newcastle Railway Station is made up of two parts. The solid exterior, built in 1863, looks like a Classical temple. Inside, the Grade 1 listed building, stone, glass and iron combine to form a majestic sweep. The walls are relatively plain, easy to ignore. Instead, it is the roof structure that astonishes: iron beams arch over the width of the platforms; above a glass clerestory lights the vast space below.

The 'Diamond Crossing' approach to Newcastle Central was at one time the largest and the busiest railway crossing in the world, and our elevated view is looking westwards into the station and gives us a hint of the amount and the variety of rail traffic it carried. The photograph from 1962 shows the 'Tyne Loop' electrified system, which was the basis of our present Metro - the Tyneside Rapid Transit System. Future years were to see many famous trains pulling into the station, with names such as 'The City of Newcastle', 'Flying Fox', 'The Flying Scotsman' and 'Silver Jubilee'. July 1927 saw hundreds of railway buffs and local officials greet 'Flying Fox' as it pulled into Central at 3.20pm, having left Kings Cross at 9.50am for the first non-stop service between London and Newcastle. During the early 1960s electric, diesel and steam trains all existed side by side, though diesel was to eventually dominate.

Right: Although it is the wrong colour, this vehicle will remind many readers of a certain age of that Flanders and Swann ditty about a 'big six wheeler, diesel engine 97 horse power omnibus'. This one was built by Northern Coachbuilders for Newcastle Corporation Transport. There are some differences from the song, as this was part of a trolleybus fleet. Introduced on 2 October, 1935, it was the start of a major winding down of the tram system that would close in 1950. In its heyday, our trolleybus service had 204 vehicles on 28 routes. The last such bus ran in 1966, on the exact 31st anniversary of the first such journey. One of the fleet can still be seen in all its yellow glory at the Beamish Open Air Museum.

corner of our street. Calling out something that vaguely sounded like 'Rabbone', housewives were quite keen to get rid of some old clothing or scraps of material in return for a donkey stone with which they could brighten up the front step. Occasionally, they could get the man to sharpen up a carving knife while their hubbies filled up a bucket at the back of the horse. Dobbin's deposits came in handy for the allotment or the rose beds.

Below: Perhaps taken in the 1970s, if we concentrate on the flared trouser bottoms for our evidence, this could be something of a Steptoe and Son situation. Whatever the case, dad and lad, for that is what they probably are, rely heavily on each other, their horse and the cart for their livelihood. There is a determined look on the faces of both humans and animal that suggests they will meet life's slings and arrows head on.

Left: This police Panda car was added to the local fleet in 1969. Patrol vehicles like this got their name from the original black and white colours in which the first cars used by the service were painted. Blue and white soon replaced these markings, but the name stuck. Lancashire Constabulary was the first to use them, doing so in 1965. The Ford Anglia was the most popular make of Panda at that time. The increased use of these vehicles is linked by many with the reduction in the numbers of bobbies on the beat.

Above: A rag and bone man is a rare sight these days. Even in 1978, this man collecting what he could on Wingrove road in Fenham, to the west of the city, was an unusual visitor. His mode of transport was not what we expected. Those of us with long memories can recall the clatter of a horse's hooves and the rattle of the wheels of the cart as the 'totter', as some knew him, came round the

WORK & INDUSTRY

THE EMPIRE
CHRISTMAS PUDDING

according to the recipe supplied by the King's Chef McCEDARD with Their Majesties Gracious Consent

1lb Currants	Australia
1lb Sultanas	Australia or South Africa
1lb Stoned Raisins	Australia or South Africa
5ozs Minced Apple	United Kingdom

Above: Apparently, according to the poster on the front of the table at this cookery demonstration held during the North East Coast Exhibition of 1929, their royal majesties, King George V and Queen Mary, had given their 'gracious consent' for the king's chef to provide Newcastle with his recipe for the grandly titled Empire Christmas Pudding. The main ingredients were listed as coming from various parts of the British Empire, with Australia and South Africa figuring prominently as contributors. The dignitary in charge of the wooden spoon does not seem as if she had practised the art of pudding stirring too often. Perhaps she still had someone below stairs who did such things for her.

Bottom left: The girls were carrying piles of invitations that were to be sent out to all readers of the Evening World. They were being asked to come along to the North East Coast Exhibition. This was a World Fair that ran from May to October in 1929. It was opened in Exhibition Park by the Prince of Wales, the future King Edward VIII, and eventually attracted 4 million visitors. It was held in an attempt to promote local industry at a time when the national economy was struggling as the start of the great depression loomed.

Below: Now then, Dobbin, wipe your feet, I have just cleaned those steps! This bizarre shot of a police horse and mounted officer, seemingly trying to enter the police station on Market Street, must have been taken no earlier than 1933 as that was the year in which this building was opened. On closer inspection, it would seem as if the woman had encouraged the horse to come up the steps as she was offering it a sugar lump or some other titbit. The British do enjoy scenes that include horses.

WALLSEND SHIPYARD

replaced its war-ravaged naval stocks. But, once that had been achieved there was a grimmer future in store for these men. Under investment and competition from the Far East reduced markets, and shipyards started to feel the pinch. By the late 1970s even the mighty Swan Hunter, also bedeviled by intransigent unions, pulled the plug and others, such as Vickers, felt the pinch. The yards at Wallsend had been an important feature in local life since Victorian times. Companies such as the Marine Steam Company, who built the experimental turbine driven 'Turbinia' in 1897, were flourishing employers. In 1906 Swan, Hunter, Richardson built the 17,000 ton 'Mauretania', Tyneside's largest vessel, but the past counts for little when the bean counters do their sums.

Left: These single deckers, the SOS IM4 and 538 dating from 1931, followed by the SE6 2 and SE4 Leylands, had no destination flagged up at the front. Just a single word, 'workmen', described the purpose of this transport. The leading bus has some form of camouflage paint on the roof in an effort to help it hide from prying eyes in the skies above. The transport fleet was taking the men off to do essential work for the war effort, but kept the actual destination a secret. The workers could have been heading for the shipyards, engineering works, armament plants or munitions factories, but wherever they were headed, the importance of their input could be guaranteed. Although there are only a handful of women to be seen in these ranks, elsewhere there would have been larger numbers undertaking vital work as they did the jobs left behind by those who had been called up into the armed forces. The photograph is undated, probably because of censorship restrictions that the government imposed to prevent valuable information leaking to the enemy. 'Be like dad, keep mum,' we were told.

Above: The men pouring out of Wallsend Shipyard on 15 October, 1957, flat caps and all, were enjoying the days of employment before the screw began to turn on the industry that had given them, and their fathers before them, a livelihood upon which they had come to rely. True, things had been difficult during the depression era of the inter-war years, but they had picked up after World War II as Britain

Below: This is one of the most modern photographs in the book. Even so, it is well over three decades old, dating from 1979. The image, though, represents an activity that is centuries old. Sarah Snowden was one of those market stall holders who plied her trade come rain or shine. Wrapped up against the elements, she portrayed a stoic figure at her pitch on Shields Road, Byker. Profits were limited in the face of competition and increasing challenges stemming from the rise in the number of supermarkets and self-service outlets. But, she battled on, as this was the only life that she knew.

Below: Men at work. Unlike the precautions taken in modern times, these workmen relied only on the protection afforded by some red and white poles and the odd red flag. Pedestrians were left to dodge the rubble as best they could, keeping one eye on the passing traffic as they did so. The scene was set along Northumberland Street in May 1957 and tremendous character is generated by the period motor cars - Austin A35s, Vauxhalls with their American styling, and a couple of snub-nosed Ford vans. Many readers will remember shopping trips to the stores seen in the background of the pictureThe 6-wheeler double-decker passing the roadworks, is advertising Fox's ginger biscuits. The biscuit manufacturer was founded in 1853, by Michael Spedding, who worked from his small bakehouse in Batley making "eatables" to sell at feasts and fairs held throughout the north of England. Apparently his daughter Hannah provided the name for the company, after she married Fred Ellis Fox in the late 1800s.

Above: These caterers' vans were built by Northern Coachbuilders (NCB) in 1938. The company occupied premises in Spital Tongues on Claremont Road. Rather oddly, it owed its existence to the tea trade. Ringston Tea Company, owned by the Smith family, delivered its goods in the early 20th century by the tried and trusted method of the horse and cart. Distribution to shops and a house-to-house service across the north of England levied a heavy demand on time and resources. The company had the foresight to embrace mechanised transport, but did so by building its own vans and lorries. The NCB was born and soon diversified into building buses, trolleybuses, mobile shops, ice cream vans and even hearses. Electric vehicles for milk rounds and bread deliveries were also added to the production line. Although the NCB is no more, the electric vehicles, branded SEV, are still made as part of the Tanfield Group.

Walter Cox
An Aladdin's Cave

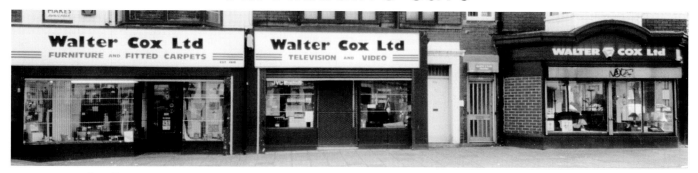

Walter Cox Ltd, on Welbeck Road, is a veritable Aladdin's cave. Customers can shop for washing machines, televisions, small electrical appliances, carpet, vinyl, prams and cots, bedroom furniture, suites, coffee tables and seasonal ranges. Always aware of client needs, Walter Cox Ltd even has a cheque cashing facility, and offers loans and gift vouchers.

The credit service can lead to some rib-tickling moments. There has been more than one occasion when the agent has knocked on a door and been greeted by a little one. When told that, "Mam's not in", the collector has asked when she will return. Having said, "I divvnt kna, hang on", the youngster gives the game away by bellowing up the stairs, "Mam, he wants to know when you'll be back"!

Walter Cox had been a watch and clock repairer before the 1914-18 war. Having served his country, he opened for business at 90, Church Street, Walker, in 1918. Walter developed a fine reputation. In 1935 the business moved to 562, Welbeck Road, and soon expanded.

The founder's son, Douglas, born in 1919, served in the armed forces during the Second World War and joined the firm on his demob.

On Walter's retirement Douglas took over. Walter's fifth son, David, born in 1946, joined the family concern on leaving school and was a director at the age of 21. By 1984 he had taken over from Douglas, who has since passed away.

Each member of staff, some of whom have been with the firm for nearly 30 years, has their own role to play, from delivering soap powder to advising which rug matches the customer's suite. It is not unusual for staff to decorate their Christmas tree, if asked!

David and his wife Kathleen have retired. The business is now run by their daughter Samantha and her partner John. Their first son arrived in June 2013, the firm's 95th anniversary: his first visit to the shop was at five days old – the next generation, who will see the business through to its 100th birthday!

Left: Walter and Ellen Cox at the wedding of Kathleen and David Cox on 6 October, 1971. Top: Cox's three shop fronts pictured in 2000. Below: A 2013 shop interior view.

Northumbrian Water
History on Tap

The 28 June, 2012, became known as 'Thunder Thursday' after a deluge of two inches of rain fell in around two hours. For Newcastle this was equivalent to the expected rainfall for the whole month. This, and further rainfall in early August, caused widespread, localised flooding incidents across the city. Further heavy rainstorms continued throughout the remainder of the year. More than 1,200 properties, including homes, businesses and schools, were affected by the summer 2012 flooding in Newcastle, with over 500 homes being flooded internally - sometimes you can have too much water!

Northumbrian Water Limited came into being in 1974 following a decision by the Government to form ten regional water authorities in England and Wales, including the Northumbrian Water Authority.

Fifteen years later, the privatisation of the water industry saw the Authority change its name to Northumbrian Water Group, and to its floating on the stock exchange.

In 1996, the giant French company, Lyonnaise des Eaux, which had earlier acquired and merged the Sunderland and South Shields Water Company and the Newcastle and Gateshead Water Company into North East Water, now bought the majority of shares in Northumbrian Water Group and merged the two companies.

The 'constantly fluid' nature of the water industry led in 2003 to SUEZ, as Lyonnaise des Eaux was now called, to sell 75% of its share holding, resulting in the company being floated again on the stock market as a FTSE 250 company and put back into British ownership. In 2005 SUEZ sold the remaining 25% of its shares.

On 14 October, 2011, Northumbrian Water Group plc (NWG), the company's controlling party at the time, was acquired by UK Water (2011) Limited (UKW). Shares in NWG were delisted from the London Stock Exchange on the same date and it was re-registered as a private limited company under the name Northumbrian Water Group Limited. UKW is now wholly owned by a consortium comprising Cheung Kong Infrastructure Holdings Limited, Cheung Kong (Holdings) Limited and Li Ka Shing Foundation Limited.

Top: A fire brigade tender from 1868, built at the suggestion of the water company. Left: The Rede Pipeline between Catcleugh and Whittle Dene in 1895. Above: Opening day at Benwell pumping station in 1903.

Today, the company serves more than 2.6 million customers in an area stretching from the Scottish borders to North Yorkshire. It is the largest environmental company in the north east of England, committed to creating a cleaner, safer and healthier environment for future generations.

At least a further 1.7 million customers in the South East also benefit from the experience of Northumbrian Water, under the brand name of Essex & Suffolk Water.

The early days of water management in Britain came at the end of the first half of the nineteenth century, a period which saw a wave of epidemic diseases, not least cholera, sweeping the country, frightening the population into questioning all aspects of sanitation. The result was the passing of the first Public Health Act 1848, although it was almost another fifty years before the authorities recognised that the problems would not be solved until the issues of sanitation in the industrial slums of major towns and cities were fully addressed.

The 1848 Act encouraged local authorities to provide a supply of constant piped water, including proper sewage and sanitary facilities to prevent contamination. Wastage or fouling of water was punishable by law.

Prior to the setting up of the Newcastle and Gateshead Water Company in 1863, William

Yarnold's Waterworks from 1697, Ralph Lodge's Waterworks until taken over by the Newcastle Fire Office in 1797, and the Subscription Water Company formed in the early years of the nineteenth century, were all involved in some sort of water supply to the people of Newcastle and Gateshead.

*Above: Fontburn viaduct construction. **Below:** An aerial view of Fontburn viaduct.*

Bateman was rejected as the engineer for the new Catcleugh development, but there were still similar quarrels about payment with engineer Thomas Hawksley, as there had been with Bateman, quarrels that continued into the new century. The Rede pipeline between Catcleugh and Whittle Dene, 30 inches in diameter and 27 miles long, was brought into use in 1895, and Catcleugh Reservoir was stocked with fish and an angling club formed.

Meanwhile, an aerial ropeway 600 yards long, crossing the Tyne from Wylam to Prudhoe and connected to a branch of the North East Railway, transported 20 tons of sand a day for the construction of new filters at Whittle Dene in 1900.

During the First World War the development of the armaments factory owned by local entrepreneur and engineer, Sir William Armstrong, caused water consumption to rise, in turn provoking the re-opening of the Wylam Pumping Station and its conversion to electricity. Further electrification followed at Barrasford, Benwell and Gateshead in the 1920s and 1930s.

In response to new legislation, the company installed the Paterson chlorine plant in 1926, and new plant was supplied to Whittle Dene in 1939.

During the Second World War the Home Guard was responsible for guarding the waterworks, whilst some staff were later sent to London to help repair the blitz-damaged mains of the Metropolitan Water Board. In 1941, Stanley George Barrett was

When the Newcastle and Gateshead Water Company was set up as one of the first water companies in England, its chairman, Richard Burdon Sanderson, was a gentleman of leisure: consequently he had plenty of time to develop the company and its services.

A reservoir was constructed at Hallington and the major issue of leakage was soon addressed. After the disastrous consequence of a fire which could not be put out due to a lack of water, Sanderson suggested that the local authority should form a fire brigade. It consisted of insurance personnel and policemen and was headed by a chief constable who was paid £20 a year.

Top left: This instrument was installed at Whittle Dene to control the flow of water. No longer in use, it was the last one in existence in the UK. **Left and below:** The opening of the new filtration works at Whittle Dene in May 1992 by HRH The Princess Royal.

Towards the end of the century, Newcastle Council considered running the water system itself, due to its concern at the area's high death rate. It decided against it. In response to a great deal of criticism of the service however, both local and governmental, improvement schemes were proposed. Colt Crag and Swinburn provided sites for new reservoirs. Mr. Bateman, an eminent engineer, responsible for the construction of the reservoir at Hallington, was employed again. Often, leakage from reservoirs occurred from fissures in the embankments due to subsidence, and repairing this damage substantially increased the cost of these facilities, but it did enable the company to supply 370,000 customers with 35 gallons of water each day.

The Northumbrian Water Authority completed the building of Kielder Reservoir in 1982, which led to the construction of Ovingham pumping station and Horsley treatment works on the River Tyne. A major new filtration system at Whittle Dene was completed in 1992.

As highlighted by the United Nations, back in 1980 when it declared a 'Decade of Water', water is an increasingly rare and threatened resource. It is something we take too much for granted and yet, it is a vital resource in the survival of mankind: we can survive three weeks without food, but after only three days without water we will die!

appointed engineer and in 1942, notices were circulated in the press encouraging the economical use of water.

The Rural Water Supply and Sewerage Act, which set £15 million aside for rural water supply, was passed in 1944. After expanding over the years into surrounding boroughs, the company realised there was an opportunity to supply the needs of the rural districts of Northumberland and, between 1950 and 1963, the company acquired the undertakings of the Castle Ward, Bellingham and nine other rural district councils.

A construction plan which eventually provided 64 service reservoirs and six treatment works for the supply of water to the rural area began in 1950. In 1952, the Coquet Water Board was formed and the River Coquet Scheme put in place in 1959. Henderson filters were installed at Throckley in 1956 and filtration work carried out at Warkworth in 1961.

WaterAid, founded in 1981, is the adopted charity of the British water industry and raises funds to finance projects in some of the poorest communities in the world in Africa, Asia, Central America and the Pacific Region, acting as a catalyst in helping communities to help themselves in water and sanitation schemes. Shocking statistics show that around 2,000 children die every day from diseases caused by dirty water and poor sanitation. More than 750 million people in the world live without safe water - this is roughly one eighth of the world's population - and 2.5 billion people live without sanitation; this is 39% of the world's population. By 2013 Northumbrian Water had contributed £5 million in fundraising for WaterAid.

*Top left: Kielder outlet. **Above:** Star Trails over Kielder captured at the Kielder Water & Forest Park observatory. **Left:** WaterAid, which works in 27 countries including parts of Africa, Asia, the Pacific region and Central America, with plans in place to expand this to 30 countries by 2015.*

Since 2002, everyone at Northumbrian Water has been able to take part in the company's 'Just an Hour' volunteering scheme. People can sign up to take part in community activities such as beach clean-ups, garden makeovers, painting and DIY at community centres or marshalling at charity events during normal working hours. Since it began, the volunteer workforce has done 82,985 hours of unpaid work for good causes. In 2012, just over 54% of the Northumbrian Water workforce participated in 'Just an Hour', supporting 695 projects.

Winter Wonderland (Christmas experience) has become a firmly established regional festive favourite, having been first launched in Kielder Water and Forest Park at Northumbrian Water's Leaplish Waterside Park in 2004. Every year, Northumbrian Water's Leaplish Waterside Park is transformed into an enchanted Winter Wonderland full of festive surprises and attractions for the whole family. Visitors can join Santa's elves in their magic workshop to help them prepare for the big day by becoming toy makers. Mrs Christmas and her friends take visitors on a glittering journey through the enchanted forest and there is also a Christmas Theatre show, skating and snow tubing. To mark the special anniversary, one of the forest's tallest pine trees was decked with Christmas lights.

One of the most popular events in the park, the Christmas experience, celebrated its tenth anniversary in 2013. Kielder Water & Forest Park was officially recognised as England's number one tourism attraction by Visit England in 2013.

After torrential rain swept away two water mains buried beneath the River Tyne at Hexham in 2005, 6,800 properties went without water for up to seven days. Northumbrian Water worked around the clock to install 5.5 km of temporary water mains in only three days. A £150,000 Pipeline Fund was set up for local community groups as a result of this incident, as a thank you to residents for their patience.

Sir Derek Wanless took over as Chairman from Sir Fred Holliday in 2007, a year in which Kielder, Northern Europe's largest man-made lake, celebrated its 25th birthday and Derwent, Northumbrian Water's second biggest reservoir, celebrated its 40th anniversary.

Top left: Volunteers at work for the 'Just an Hour' scheme. Left: Kielder Winter Wonderland is the enchanting Santa experience that keeps amazing children who visit the festive forest and lakeside landscape. With a variety of activities throughout the day, the experience is sure to be as action packed as it is magical. Above: Facing the challenges of climate change. Flooding in the Tyne Valley in 2005 – picture courtesy of the Hexham Courant.

A mains cleaning programme got underway in Newcastle in 2008 to ensure water quality in the city and the River Tyne voted Best Salmon River in England and Wales after the river clean-up. Northumbrian Water's corporate partners of major regional institutions include Tyne and Wear Museums, the Sage, Tyne Theatre and the Baltic. Sponsorship of events has included the University Boat Race, the Tall Ships Race and the Evolution Festival.

Kielder Observatory was opened in 2008 by Sir Arnold Wolfendale, the 14th Astronomer Royal. About 200 public events a year are delivered by the Kielder Observatory Astronomy Society and a team of passionate volunteers, at what is the only purpose-built observatory in a truly dark sky location in the whole of Europe.

In 2009, Northumbrian Water was one of 12 companies nationally to receive the Queen's Award for Enterprise and the only company in the North East to be recognised in this category.

Heidi Mottram OBE was appointed as Chief Executive Officer in 2010, having moved from Northern Rail Limited where she was Managing Director for five years. Earlier that year she was named Rail Business Manager of the Year at the annual Rail Business Awards for being "an inspirational leader who makes a huge personal difference to passengers and employees." Heidi took up the position at Northumbrian Water following the retirement of John Cuthbert.

Northumbrian Water was recognised as one of the world's most responsible companies in 2011, earning a place on the Ethisphere Institute's World's Most Ethical Companies list. World-wide there were only 110 companies on the list, only five UK-based companies and, of these, Northumbrian Water was the only UK utility to be listed.

Today, Northumbrian Water continues to lead the way in innovative technology and as a guardian of the environment.

The Advanced Anaerobic Digestion (AAD) plant at Howdon, North Tyneside is one of the company's two hi-tech plants that turn sludge left over from sewage treatment into electricity that powers the site. The company has also pioneered the use of drinking-water sludge to make building bricks, and is working closely with scientists at Newcastle University to develop DNA fingerprinting of bacteria in sewage to learn more about potential future uses for recycled waste water.

Above: *The Kielder Water & Forest Park observatory.*
Below: *Howdon AAD gas bags*

Miller UK
A History of Innovation

Miller UK Ltd was founded in 1978 as a mobile welding and repair service for quarries, mines and open cast coal sites. Today the firm operates on a global basis. The main manufacturing site is in Cramlington, but it also supplies the latest in coupler technology from a joint venture casting facility in Northern China.

From both sites Miller manufactures a range of buckets, quick couplers and other attachments for the earthmoving industries, as well as providing specialised and 'one off' products, tailor-made to suit specific applications.

Customers include the world's leading names such as Volvo, JCB, CNH, Komatsu, and their dealer networks, as well as an established independent global distributor network.

Though steam power was used for moving earth and rock in the 19th century it was the early years of the 20th which witnessed the start of a revolution. Between 1904 and 1914 the Americans showed how it could be done when they used massive steam powered cranes and excavators to claw out the 50-mile length of the Panama Canal. It would, however, not be until after the Second World War that caterpillar-tracked mobile cranes and excavators would become an everyday sight. But excavators bring their own problems. At times whatever is at the end of an excavator's

powerful arm needs to be changed: often because being quite literally at the sharp end of operations, they inevitably get damaged - but equally it is often simply to change the type of attachment. Yet the growth in the use of various attachments to the arms of hydraulic excavators had not been matched by the ease with which they could be changed. Talk to any excavator operator in the 1970s and one of his biggest complaints would have been the time-consuming business of changing from bucket to bucket or from bucket to rock breaker.

Though several makes of quick coupler would eventually appear on the market, one which would offer unique advantages was produced in Newcastle upon Tyne by Miller UK Ltd.

Since the firm's first bucket (made in 1979 for National Smokeless Fuels at Lampton Coke Works) the name Miller has become famed within the industry for its honest, no nonsense approach to its business, and for listening to its customers.

But how did it all start?

In 1978 a keen young man left his safe job and started out on his own, offering an onsite mobile welding service to local quarries, mines, open cast coal sites and plant hire companies. The boss of the welding company he had left told the

Top left: A young Gary Miller inside a face shovel bucket repaired by his own fair hand. *Centre:* Men at work on a Marrion face shovel refurbishment. *Below:* Miller's mobile welding service.

wheeled loading shovels: now for the first time the company exhibited its products at the National Exhibition Centre in Birmingham, attended by Keith, Gary and their younger sister Jacqui.

As enquiries increased for Miller products and services Jacqui Miller joined her brothers, helping promote the Miller name throughout the construction industry countrywide.

Due to increasing sales a move was made to larger premises in Newcastle's Skinnerburn Road where there was enough space to meet the needs imposed by an expanding order book. Not only did demand continue to rise from the construction sector, but sales now began to grow to the quarry and mining sectors, as well as the company offering bucket and attachment repairs to all the well-known makes of earth moving equipment.

young Keith Miller, 'There's no real chance of promotion in the foreseeable future', but generously added, 'Your job is always here if you go bust'.

Happily it didn't take Keith Miller, then just 21, long to secure a regular stream of work from the North East's construction industry - not least an important contract to maintain the plant at the Kielder Dam project.

"I knew I was a good welder" Keith would recall. "Many customers asked for me by name; or for the 'the tall skinny lad' as I was back then. After canvassing a few of them I decided I could make a living even if I didn't have a van. I sold my precious Starsky & Hutch style Ford Granada and bought a second hand Ford Escort estate car for £295 at a local auction".

Armed with a Mighty Midgit welding set, Keith was in business.

The next year, 1979, Keith's brother Gary, aged just 18, joined him and together they operated out of their rented allotment which cost them £5 a month. They soon acquired their first factory at Tower Street on Newcastle Quayside.

With their strong work ethic the pair offered a 24-hour a day, seven days a week service. To keep up with demand the duo soon found themselves having to employ a small team of local welders and fabricators, and a new name: Miller Welding Engineers.

By 1981 the Miller brothers had moved from simple welding repairs, to the manufacture of buckets for hydraulic excavators and for

By the middle of the 1980s the Millers realised how important it was to raise the company's business profile. Ways of promoting the business included attending exhibitions, sending out mailshots, telephoning potential customers, as well as advertising in the press. It was as a result of attending an exhibition in 1988 that a partnership was established which changed the growing company's future direction remarkably.

*Top left: Miller's former Skinnerburn Road premises. **Below:** Keith, Jacqui and Gary Miller attending their first International Exhibition in Paris, France.*

The company now entered into a relationship with a contracting company that was developing the idea of a quick and efficient method of changing excavator buckets without the need for the operator to leave his cab. The Quick Coupler concept originated in New Zealand, however, it was Keith and brother Gary along with the team at Miller who developed the design into the Mag 7 coupler (so named because it reduced bucket and attachment changeover to a Magnificent 7 seconds). This revolutionary product was launched into the UK construction and associated industries in 1989.

This method of changing buckets and attachments saved operators millions of hours in otherwise unproductive down time, and in the process increased profits and saved machine owners millions of pounds.

Demand for the Miller Quick Coupler soared. The company was soon able to invest in further product development. Having helped others become more productive they wanted to be more productive themselves. In late 1991 the Millers were visited by the famous 'trouble-shooter' Sir John Harvey Jones who gave

them two pieces of advice 'Sort out your production flow' and 'Get into Europe'.

As winners of the 1994 Small Business of the Year award, the Miller trio's confidence soared and armed with a business plan which called for production to treble in three years, the production flow problems were sorted out in a much larger factory and stockyard than the company had ever had before, and distributors had been taken on in France and Italy. Further European countries would be next.

As demand continued to grow, the company was approached by Caterpillar to develop a truly universal and fully automatic coupler solution to fit their varying range, of excavators. The hydraulic coupler was operated from a simple switch inside the excavator cab. The system allowed an experienced operator to change over from one attachment to another in seconds. Even better, the system could be fitted to any excavator in only a few hours without the need to alter the machine's hydraulics system. A busy machine carrying out a variety of work on a construction site might need to change attachments five or more times a day. Without a quick coupler that could mean an excavator driver spending up to two hours on the unproductive task of removing and refitting pins.

The company celebrated its 20th anniversary in 1998 with a £1.75 million investment in new plant and machinery, expanding into a second factory at Blaydon, North East England in preparation for an anticipated surge in demand for its products and services, not least from the USA. In March 1999, at Conexpo, an international exhibition held every three years in Las Vegas, another milestone in the Company's history was reached at the signing of a global contract with construction equipment manufacturing giant, Caterpillar inc. of North America.

Top left: *One of the very first Miller Quick Couplers.* **Above:** *Above right: Keith, Jacqui and Gary Miller with 'Troubleshooter' Sir John Harvey Jones.* **Left:** *By 2003 Miller had acquired this facility on an 18 acre site which afforded ample opportunity for further expansion.*

bespoke solutions to individual customers own specifications anywhere in the world, in addition to managing the repair and servicing of buckets and attachments.

Continuing improvements to products, and the introduction of novel solutions would help fuel customers' growth through improved productivity, for example Miller's Scoop System designed for hydraulic excavators. Using the Scoop System customers could increase productivity by up to 25 per cent.

At the start of the 21st century, as pioneers of the pin pick-up hydraulic quick coupler system and with continual reinvestment, Miller UK Ltd and its management team maintained the company's position as the market leader and aimed to be the premier bucket and coupler manufacturer worldwide. This mission was well on the way to being achieved as the firm became the only pin pick-up manufacturer to supply the world's leading OEMs (Original Equipment Manufacturers), namely CAT, JCB, Komatsu, CNH and Volvo.

By the end of the 20th century the company had more than 200 employees, three manufacturing sites in and around Blaydon and offices in Germany, China and Japan. More and more companies specified the Miller Quick Coupler as standard, that choice being driven by the need to use the right-sized attachment every time and recognition that quality remains key in an ever competitive market.

Though at its outset the business may have been a one man band, by the opening years of the 21st century the company was split into three divisions: Quick Coupler manufacture, hydraulic excavator bucket manufacture, and a specialist products division. The specialist division is dedicated to offering

Top left: Jacqui Miller & Kunal Mehta on site in India with coupler 2010. Centre: CAT 785 dump truck at shot BANKS Mining, an example of Miller's repair service. Below: A view inside the facility at bucket production line.

By the end of 2003 the company completed another factory relocation, to a significantly larger facility set in 18 acres of land in Cramlington just outside Newcastle. This 150,000 ft² facility amalgamated all three existing production units under one roof, and not only further streamlined the manufacturing processes but afforded Miller the space to further expand. The Cramlington factory was officially opened by both HRH The Duke of Kent and Sir Digby Jones, Director General of the CBI, now Lord Jones of Birmingham.

In 2005 a CJV was formed with it steel casting partner, and Miller Construction Machinery Co Ltd was established with its foundry located in northern China. The company casts couplers on a large scale and component coupler parts for its international sales distribution. This allows Miller to supply a more extensive global market with a consistent, high quality, reliable product.

The following year saw the launch of Miller's mini product range, now offering solutions for machines as small as one tonne up to 140 tonne excavators.

As the business turned 30 it was commemorated by a 'Pearl Ball', attended by the outgoing CBI Director General, Sir Digby

Jones. The evening was a great success, and friends, family, customers and stakeholders helped to raise almost £30k for the company's chosen charity, the NSPCC.

The successful growth the company had enjoyed over the last decade was to come to an abrupt end during the 2nd quarter of the 2008 trading year. A global economic crisis loomed, the likes of which the world had never seen. Miller was just one of many millions of companies caught up in the catastrophic turmoil which led to difficult decisions being made to cut the workforce by two-thirds. Survival mode was very much the new way of thinking. The industry struggled to recover, 2009 marked one of the bleakest periods in the Company's history as sales and morale plummeted to an all-time low.

Born and bred in the North East, survival instincts are part of the business DNA and through a sheer determination to succeed at all costs along with hard work, lots of sleepless nights and commitment from the remaining Miller employees, the business began its road to recovery and in January 2012 with the signing of a new North American partner the future looked brighter.

Despite the recession, Miller took the brave step of opening an India office in late 2009, always a company with vision the company recognised the opportunity the market offered longer term and chose to invest into the future.

The Miller TwinLock - the first ever twin locking coupler – was also invented in 2011. The design has since morphed into what is now the company's flagship coupler, the PowerLatch. In 2013 Miller Mate was launched, another innovation from Miller's R&D team eliminating accidental release to avoid injury to ground workers.

Top left: Great buckets from Great Britain, the team at Hillhead in 2012. *Left:* Miller's gigantic PC 4000 Bucket - a bulk handling bucket manufactured for Komatsu USA, for use in coal mining in Canada. *Above:* Miller UK factory, Cramlington 2013.

In addition, 2013 saw the establishment of Miller Australia PYT Ltd as well as the appointment of new distributors in Indonesia, Qatar and Oman.

The executive board still contains its three founders: Chairman, Keith Miller, Technical Director Gary Miller and Sales and Marketing Director Jacqui Miller, who was appointed a Member of the British Empire (MBE) for services to industry and international trade in the 2013 New Year Honours List.

The success of the company has only been achieved by the consistent investment in current product as well as dedication to innovation. In an increasingly competitive marketplace, this investment is what helps Miller differentiate from its competitors.

Keith Miller, founder and Chairman has no doubts as to what has made the firm the success story it is. He says "We have stayed true to our roots, invested in our people and worked hard to export quality products to a global customer based from our North East home."

How did they do it? The Millers put it down to a philosophy of 'The Three Ps' - people, products and performance. The right people ensure that the correct products are supplied, which in turn perform to the customer's expectations. In pursuit of that philosophy the company has a continuing programme of staff training running alongside ongoing research directed specifically at developing new cost effective products. Those who once used picks and spades must have blessed the inventor of the mechanical shovel. Since those days excavator drivers must have equally often blessed the name of Miller.

Left: Keith Miller, Jacqui Miller and Gary Miller. **Above:** Jacqui Miller receives her MBE for services to industry, 2013. **Below:** A group photo to celebrate Miller's 35th Anniversary, 2013.

Ringtons
Time and Tea

Ringtons, the renowned British tea and coffee merchant, has over a century of experience in providing the highest quality tea, coffee and biscuits to customers all over the world.

Founded in the Edwardian era by Samuel Smith in Newcastle upon Tyne, horse and carts once delivered tea to the doorsteps of customers all over the region. Today, the iconic horse and cart have long since been swapped for modern vans which deliver to over 260,000 customers all over the UK, while an ecommerce website delivers worldwide. The company remains a family business, and is now headed by the fourth generation of the founding family.

Established in 1907, Ringtons started life when Samuel Smith, born in 1872, moved from his home in Leeds and began selling tea from a horse and cart to the households of Heaton in Newcastle upon Tyne.

Sam began with an initial investment of just £250 from business partner William Titterington. Contrary to popular belief, there never was a Mr Rington - the name 'Ringtons' was formed from the last half of William's surname and the 'S' from Smith.

With a focus on a quality doorstep delivery service, the business soon flourished. Sam moved to larger premises, buying out William's share of the business in 1914. Ringtons truly became a family business when Sam's son Douglas joined, starting as a van boy.

It was, however, to be a tough period for Ringtons; many employees were sent to fight in the First World War, whilst at home rationing and new sales laws were put into force. The business had to diversify into other food stuff.

*Top: Founder, Samuel Smith. **Left and below:** Ringtons delivery vehicles parked outside the company premises before (left) and after the extension (below) in 1914.*

In a desperate attempt to survive Sam Smith sold anything he could get, including dried eggs, baking powder, canned meats, fish and pickles.

There was a rebirth of the business after 1918. A total of 48 depots were opened, and wherever possible Sam employed ex-service men. To house the booming business Sam opened a new, purpose-built, six-storey head office and factory on Algernon Road in Byker, Newcastle upon Tyne, in 1926.

In the early 1920s Ringtons also bought two motorised vehicles to assist with deliveries; but it seemed the Geordie housewives preferred their brew to be brought by traditional horse and cart (it wasn't until over 40 years later that Monty, the last horse finally retired).

Ringtons is known for the range of ceramic products it has sold over the years, including the popular Chintz and Willow pattern. The first Ringtons piece was commissioned in 1929 from the Maling Pottery in Newcastle.

The Cathedral and Bridges jars were very popular with customers, and were soon followed by the highly-collectable blue floral Chintz teapots of the early 1930s.

More growth for Ringtons came in the 1930s when Sam returned to his native Leeds, where he demolished his former home and built a brand new Ringtons factory.

Above: One of the company's early motorised vehicles. **Below left:** Monty, the last of the Ringtons horses pictured before his retirement in 1967. **Bottom:** Ringtons six-storey head office and factory on Algernon Road. **Right:** Ringtons popular blue floral Chintz teapot and plate of the early 1930s.

The building still stands today as a Sikh temple: the original Ringtons engravings can be seen on the exterior.

During that decade, the 'hungry-thirties', Ringtons staff enjoyed day trips to Scarborough. Special free trains were arranged to take staff and their families to the seaside for the day; the outings were a thank-you from the Smiths. Judging from photos in the Ringtons' archive it looked like a jolly good day out!

Sam Smith, however, went even further afield, visiting India and Ceylon (Sri Lanka) in 1935. On his return he published a report of his trip in the house magazine 'The Ringtonian': "Having recently returned from a visit to India and Ceylon in company with my youngest son, Malcolm (hereinafter referred to as Mac) I have been asked by several people to give a talk on our experiences and impressions during that visit. Not being a Public Speaker I think the best thing is for me to make use of the 'Ringtonian' and to give extracts from the Diary which I diligently kept through the trip, so that those who are interested may read and those not interested may not be bored by listening to a talk.

"Mac having recently completed his training in our Sale room and two years in a London Sale Room, we considered it wise for him to see the cultivation and manufacturing side of tea before taking up a position in the firm as Assistant Buyer. His brother, Douglas, did the trip about five years ago and I consider the cost was money well spent. I have had over 53 years in the trade but never had those advantages so I decided to accompany Mac.

"I had read many books on tea cultivation but never visualised the various processes exactly as we found them carried out. Ceylon is a beautiful country - India is vast and wonderful - 400 million population. The British have done great things for India and a great deal more has to be done. To hand the country over to the agitators for Home Rule would prove a terrible calamity to India. Ceylon has a kind of Home Rule and although it is British capital and British enterprise that has built up the industries of the Island (tea principally) the Cingalese will buy from anyone in preference to the British. If Britain cut them off entirely they would be annexed by Japan very quickly and it would serve them right too."

Attitudes have since changed!

*Top: The Ringtonians staff dance, 1929. **Centre:** Early Ringtons advertising. **Below:** Samuel Smith (seated front) and family.*

Renowned for quality and strength, Ringtons tea was growing in popularity, so much so that the company commissioned its own special song 'The Vocal One Step'. Alas, the good times were once more about to end.

In the 1940s Ringtons was again seriously affected by war. Over 400 employees, including Samuel's four grandsons, were called up to fight in the Second World War. By 1943 some 200 vans were taken off the road. Sam donated his own car to the ambulance corps. Once again, however, determination and the Ringtons' spirit triumphed, and the business kept going.

Most of those who served in the forces, including Sam's grandsons, returned to work for the company after the war. Samuel Smith was not to witness the historic changes that were to follow in the post war era. He died on 12 August, 1949, aged 77.

Sam had been noted throughout the north as one of its most generous benefactors, with gifts to struggling organisations and needy charities. His will left sons Douglas and Malcolm with shares in the business. At the age of 50, it was Douglas who took over the tea business, to be joined later by his sons Douglas Jnr, Norman and Johnnie.

By 1954 all but one of Ringtons door-to-door delivery rounds were being made by motor vehicles. What was once a small tea delivery service was now an incredibly successful family business.

In 1961 Ringtons even aired a TV advert. Cliff Taylor rolled up his trousers and waded across to St Mary's Lighthouse in Ringtons' first television commercial. With a focus on increasing customer awareness the advertisements were shown across the Tyne Tees region.

With the customers' convenience in mind, Ringtons introduced the very first tea bag machine to the factory at Algernon Road in 1964. Tea bags are taken for granted today, but previously tea had been sold and used as loose leaf. Tea bags were easier to use and did away with the need for strainers.

Kept for sentimental reasons, Ringtons' last horse, Monty, was retired to green pastures in 1967 after conditions on the road became too busy to accommodate horses safely. A popular Ringtons' icon, the horse and cart was celebrated with the Monty soft toy: it proved to be a big hit with customers and staff alike.

Top left: Members of the team sampling tea. *Centre:* A post-war Ringtons tea salesman and company vehicle. *Left:* Ringtons first tea bag machine. *Below:* Inside the packaging department in the 1960s.

supply of its favourite blends to customers. The crisis caused tea prices to soar, but using its buying and blending expertise, Ringtons was still able to maintain quality.

Meanwhile, with increased demand in the south, new offices were opened to cope with the requests from growing customer numbers. A brand new warehouse facility near Pontefract was opened to handle teas from India, Kenya and Sri Lanka. With a capacity for holding 1,100 tonnes of tea, the business was ready for the increased demand.

With the retirement of John (Jonnie) Smith in the mid-1980s, the 4th generation of Smiths was handed the managerial mantle; they soon set in motion their plans to streamline the business. New packing techniques at the tea estates, introduced in the 1990s, allowed Ringtons to deliver a truly fresh cup of tea from tea gardens in Kenya and India. Packing the tea in airtight foil containers to retain that 'just picked' taste proved very successful.

Douglas's son Johnnie took over at Ringtons in 1972. When he began this new role his eldest son Nigel also joined the business as a Trainee Buyer.

In 1975 Ringtons won an account to supply to Marks and Spencer (which it continues to do today). The decade was rounded off in 1979 by a VIP visit to Algernon Road from none other than 'Iron Lady' Margaret Thatcher. The Conservative leader told of her preference for tea bags, noting they are "much more convenient". (For a lady with such a busy lifestyle, we're not surprised)!

Growing demand put increased pressure on the factory at Algernon Road. Built in 1929 and expanded on a number of occasions, it simply wasn't big enough to cope with the increased volume of tea. A new custom-built factory was erected at Balliol Park in 1995 to produce all Ringtons' tea products.

Nigel's brothers Simon and Colin joined the business in the 1980s and were able to gain valuable and expert knowledge from all over the globe. When the world was sent into turmoil by the tea export embargo from India in 1983 Ringtons was still able to ensure a continuous

Soft tea packs, reminiscent of the old style tea products produced by Sam Smith in 1907, replaced boxes when the factory team developed a new tea packing format in 2000. They would ensure the freshest taste and protect the tea on its journey to the customer. By the end of 2004, the days of writing out all the transactions in sales books had gone completely. Every office was equipped with its own set of hand-held computers.

Top left: Colin, Simon and Nigel Smith, fourth generation of the Smith family. Centre: Former Prime Minister, Margaret Thatcher, visits Ringtons in 1979. Left: A selection of products including Ringtons popular Extra Fresh and Kenyan Gold.

At the same time, the tea-buying team was introducing 'supplier partnership' with key growers in Kenya and India to ensure the consistency and quality of Ringtons tea.

Ringtons Beverages was founded 30 years ago as the business-to-business division of the company. Ringtons Beverages supplies a catering and business audience with the best quality tea, coffee, barista equipment, barista supplies, edibles, crockery, and catering items.

It is important for Ringtons, as a brand and as a sustainable business, to accurately monitor suppliers' commitment to human rights, good employment conditions, and ethical business practices.

Ringtons has a core group of suppliers from whom it has been buying for more than thirty years, and with whom it has very good, strong relationships. As business has grown, Ringtons has had to expand its supply base, but its ethical principles have remained important in these new trading relationships.

The company is still concerned about the traceability of its teas and about good employment conditions, human rights and ethical business practices at every stage of the supply chains, and has therefore joined the Ethical Tea Partnership (ETP). This organisation conducts social accountability audits on tea estates on behalf of its members and shares this information between them.

In the company's centenary year, 2007, Ringtons was awarded the Honorary Freedom of the City of Newcastle.

Ringtons took the strategic decision to expand the business through franchising in 2009, creating opportunities for anyone wishing to start their own business. Franchisees now have the opportunity to replicate Ringtons' successful, century-old, formula in their local town and communities, building businesses through personal service and excellent customer relationships.

Looking ahead to the future the company's famous packaging underwent a complete overhaul in 2013; the first in 15 years and only the third since the 1960s. The new packaging commemorates the rich heritage and expertise of Ringtons whilst incorporating modern styling in a move which unifies the wide range of items on offer, gives customers more information to help them make the right choices and sets this unique company apart in the competitive tea and coffee marketplace, as it has been since those early days in 1907.

A truly remarkable family business.

Top left: Tea and more to your door - Ringtons doorstep service. *Top right:* On a tea estate is Assam *Centre:* Colin Smith, Tea Packing Division Director and great-grandson of Ringtons founder Samuel Smith and Lisa Thornton, Head of Marketing launch the company's new packaging which commemorates the rich heritage and expertise of Ringtons whilst incorporating modern styling. *Below:* A recent view inside Ringtons production facility.

Nixon Hire
Family Values

Nixon Hire, the trading name of John Nixon Ltd, is a leading provider of plant and site equipment, with bases throughout the United Kingdom and even further afield.

Founded in 1967, Nixon Hire is a dynamic and professional family-run business employing over 330 people across all of many its sites.

Nixon Hire draws on decades of experience to deliver quality, products and services that are second to none from its large headquarters in Scotswood Road, Newcastle-upon-Tyne, and its numerous bases throughout northern England and Scotland.

Today, the company specialises in a number of business sectors: non-operated plant hire, tool and equipment hire, temporary accommodation hire, toilet hire, new plant and part sales, used plant sales, liquid waste removal, and plant repairs and maintenance.

With many years of experience in its industry, the company aims to provide a one-stop-shop for construction plant related products with excellent customer service. The company is fully committed to offering the best service in the industry and is completely dedicated to offering the highest quality products.

An ongoing fleet investment programme ensures that Nixon Hire operates one of the youngest hire fleets in the UK today, meaning that their equipment is extremely reliable and suffers fewer breakdowns. Being distributors for only leading brands of equipment ensures that the company not only obtains plant at the most competitive terms, but also benefits its service in the respect that it stocks new machines which can be added to the hire fleet at a moment's notice. The firm also holds spare parts so that machine downtimes are kept to an absolute minimum in the event that parts are required.

Above: Founder, John Nixon, pictured in the early days. **Below left:** *Where it all began, the first premises in Back New Bridge Street.* **Below:** *A company price list from 1971.*

Hiring quality equipment is one thing, service and support another, however, it is people that really make a difference. Nixon Hire firmly believes in exceeding customer expectations in terms of outstanding customer service. That goal can only be achieved by employing people with the right attitude, knowledge, experience and commitment.

The company aims to develop long-term business relationships with each of its customers, and offer a completely flexible approach that is so refreshing in this day and age of faceless business.

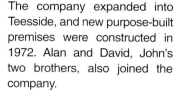

Nixon Hire are also keen to embrace new technology. It operates a modern and sophisticated hire system, utilises state of the art PDAs, advance route planning software and has a strong presence on social media sites such as Facebook and Twitter. Such things could only be dreamed of when the firm was founded.

John Nixon Ltd was incorporated by John Nixon in December 1967. The company's headquarters (then barely big enough to service a few machines at a time) were situated in Back New Bridge Street, Newcastle upon Tyne.

John employed a fitter while he toured Northern England and Scotland providing a repair service. Sales enquiries, however, soon began to come in and John Nixon Ltd became a distributor for a number of leading plant manufacturers.

The company expanded into Teesside, and new purpose-built premises were constructed in 1972. Alan and David, John's two brothers, also joined the company.

By 1974 annual turnover had reached £1.25 million. and the company moved to Water Street in Newcastle.

A depot of the company was opened in Edinburgh in 1981.

John Nixon Ltd purchased the plant division of Stanley Miller in 1987. This acquisition included 70 second-hand steel security containers. Soon after this the company began to manufacture these containers. Welders and joiners were recruited to complete this phase of the company's growth.

Above: The team at an early trade show. *Below:* At work inside the Water Street premises in the 1970s.

Over the next two years demand for plant and equipment spread to cable and utility companies. The company's reputation for quality and excellence helped lead the way in this field. National investment in cable television and the communication infrastructure at this time helped Nixon Hire to gain respect on a national scale and become an important supply chain partner for many large customers.

After winning a cable contract in the Leeds/Bradford area, the company opened a Bradford depot in 1997.

John's five children had all joined the business in the early 1990s and set up Nixon Site Services Ltd. Having received enquiries for portable flushing toilets, the site service arm of the business bought 25 units and began hiring them out with great success. Demand grew and so did their supply of units. As John's children gained valuable business experience, the company's vehicle hire fleet also expanded to boast an 800 strong fleet of vans.

As the company came out of the recession in the early nineties, the demand for construction equipment boomed. Nixon Hire was able to expand its services with a full range of small tools, plant, accommodation, vehicles and portable toilets.

In 1994, the family sold the vehicle hire side of the business in order to focus on construction plant and equipment hire and sales. Proceeds from the sale of the vehicle hire business were invested in a Sunderland depot, opening in October 1994.

The Bradford depot was relocated to a larger depot on a two acre site off Leeds Road, Bradford, in 1999, followed a year later by the opening of a depot in Perth.

A defining year in the company's history was 2005. Not only did the company install a state-of-the-art hire management system across all depots, but new depots opened simultaneously in Dundee and Aberdeen on the demise of Cox Hire. Cox staff were employed by Nixon Hire, with many still working for the company today. In the same year, the toilet hire division of Owen Pugh was acquired, adding further depots at Glasgow and Cupar, in Fife, with toilets in North East England being incorporated into existing depots.

Top left: *An early John Nixon transit van on the road to Scotland.* **Left:** *Members of the Nixon family outside the new purpose-built premises in 1974. Left to right: Alan Nixon, David Nixon, Thelma Nixon, John Nixon and Jack Nixon.* **Above:** *The new premises and plant for hire.*

In May of 2006 the company commenced trading from Carlisle, giving it a presence in Cumbria, Lancashire and Dumfriesshire. Later that year the company opened a Toilet Hire depot in Liverpool.

The company gained full accreditation to ISO 9001 quality standard across all depots in 2007. Meanwhile, a Wakefield depot was opened and new premises in Sunderland were purchased, greatly enhancing service there.

Nixon Hire Middle East was created in 2009 with the opening of an office in Doha, Qatar. Nixon eXtra was also createdto allow the company to offer a truly national service with carefully selected service partners across the UK.

Nixon eXtra developed several standalone websites to capitalise on the growth opportunities from the internet, initially focusing on toilet hire with new sites and product lines rolled out regularly thereafter.

The creation of Nixon Direct followed, a team designed to provide tailored service solutions and one point of contact for larger customers.

The Aberdeen operation relocated to larger premises in 2010. A new range of Welfare Vans was introduced to the hire fleet, bringing vehicles back to the fleet after a sixteen year absence. Welfare vans continue to provide a flexible approach to short term site accommodation and deliver comfortable and cost effective welfare facilities. The vans include a canteen equipped with a microwave, running hot water, a full size sink as well as a unisex toilet and drying facilities.

Expansion in Scotland continued with an Inverness depot opening in March 2011, extending coverage across North West Scotland. Despite the most difficult trading conditions in decades, the company launched an ambitious business plan, split into phases to the year 2020. The plan is aptly named '2020 Vision'.

The company relocated its Central Support Office to new premises on Scotswood Road, Newcastle, in 2012, whilst the consolidation of three depots (Cupar, Perth & Dundee) into one large hub depot in Dundee was finalised.

Top: A Nixon vehicle en route in Newcastle in the early 1980s. *Left:* Equipment Nixon Hire Middle East supplied to the Khalifa Stadium, Aspire Complex for the Pan Arab Games. *Centre:* A Nixon Hire Welfare Van.

Embracing new technology, the Nixon Hire iPhone App was launched in 2012, featuring the online catalogue in an easy to navigate and a convenient format.

2013 would be an extremely busy year for the company. It would open a 2.5 acre site in Warrington offering all of its core products, including plant, accommodation, toilets and welfare vans. The company also invested over £19 million in its hire fleet resulting in 400 accommodation units, 62 Volvo excavators, 120 Bomag rollers, 400 portable toilets, 90 new welfare vans, 107 JCB telehandlers and 21 other vehicles.

The company is incredibly proud of the fact that in such difficult economic times, they have been able to create jobs for over 30 people since January 2013. The roles come as a direct result of company growth and investment and cover a range of positions from apprentices to senior management. The jobs come as a direct result of company growth and investment and cover a range of positions from apprentices to senior management.

Today, from Inverness in the north to Wakefield and Warrington in the south, Nixon Hire's depot network is expanding continually to cover Scotland, northern England, and beyond.

Despite the most difficult economic trading conditions the company has ever encountered from late 2008 and 2009, turnover continues to grow at an impressive rate, with 15% growth in 2010, 2011 and 2012 and double digit growth in 2013.

The company is widely recognised as one of the fastest growing plant hire companies in the UK and has one of the most modern fleets available. Nixon Hire is also proud to have been one of the top 50 fastest growing companies in the North East of England for three consecutive years.

The toilet division of the company is widely acclaimed, and has provided hundreds of toilets for events such as The Great North Run, Reading Festival, Leeds Festival, Love Parade, Creamfields, Princes Trust and T in the Park in Scotland.

Since it was founded in 1967 the company has won many awards over the years and is now one of the top ten largest privately-owned plant hire companies in the UK. It is also one of the largest family run businesses of its kind.

Top: Nixon Hire plant on site. **Centre:** A map detailing the Nixon Hire depot network and dates formed. **Left:** Nixon Hire Central Support Office at Citywest Business Park, Scotswood Road, Newcastle on Tyne.

with two depots planned for Saudi Arabia in Jeddah and Riyadh. In 2013 the company spent over £19m on new products for its hire fleet, and looks forward to the future investing in its people, processes and products for many years to come.

Meanwhile, as a family business, the company understands the collective energy, drive and enthusiasm of its people can have a positive impact on the wider community.

The company works closely with its chosen charity throughout each year to do as much as it can to raise money as well as awareness for the important causes it supports. In addition to fundraising events, the company also supports many registered charities each year by offering discounted prices on hire products when supplied to charity events.

Nixon Hire's chosen charity for 2013 was Cancer Research UK, with fundraising totalling over £30,000 - a remarkable achievement.

John Nixon, the company founder, is Chairman. Chris and Graham Nixon are joint Managing Directors. Alison Blackwood (nee Nixon) and Beverley Brown (nee Nixon) are HR Directors. Alison's husband, Kevin Blackwood, is Director of Sales, whilst Graham's wife, Ashleigh Nixon, is Commercial Manager of Nixon Direct.

For the future Nixon Hire is continuing with its plans for expansion and will be opening further depots in the Middle East,

Top: Happy staff pictured after completing the Ben Nevis Charity Challenge climb in September 2013. **Above left and inset:** *Nixon Hire unveil the Nixon Hire Cancer Research excavator, pictured inset.* **Below:** *The Nixon family, 2013, from left: John, Chris, Graham, Beverly and Alison.*

Northern Powergrid
Powering the Region

Northern Powergrid runs the major electricity distribution network that delivers power to the vast majority of customers in the Northeast, Yorkshire and northern Lincolnshire. The company doesn't sell electricity, neither does it operate power stations. But it does operate a network of more than 61,000 substations and around 91,000 kilometres of overhead power lines and underground cables that takes electricity from National Grid's transmission network and from smaller generators and delivers it to 3.9 million homes and businesses throughout the region.

NESCo, the original company which would evolve to become Northern Powergrid, was a pioneer in both power generation and supply. The electricity industry was nationalised in 1948, and in this region the North Eastern Electricity Board (NEEB) replaced NESCo and a number of smaller private and municipal suppliers. In 1989, however, as part of the privatisation of the industry, NEEB became Northern Electric and was floated on the stock exchange.

In 1996 Northern Electric became part of the world energy group CalEnergy, which, renamed as MidAmerican Energy Holdings Company, is now part of Warren Buffett's Berkshire Hathaway group of companies. But where did it all start?

The North East of England was at the forefront of developments in electricity - Joseph Swan invented the electric light bulb and gave its first public demonstration to the Newcastle Chemical Society in 1878. Lord Armstrong installed Swan's lights in Cragside Hall powered by the first domestic hydro-electric generator in 1880. And Charles Parsons invented the first steam turbine in Newcastle, where it was soon used to generate electricity.

Top left: Joseph Swan's incandescent lamp, first demonstrated to the Newcastle Chemical Society in 1878. ***Above:*** *Pandon Dene Generating Station which began supplying electricity for NESCo in 1890.* ***Below:*** *The Travelling Showroom arrives at an outlying electrified village in the 1920s.*

Newcastle upon Tyne and District Electric Lighting Company (DISCo) also being formed in 1889. DISCo was owned by Charles Parsons whose steam turbine generators were installed at Forth Banks by the river.

The generating station at Pandon Dene consisted of two small 75 kilowatt generators. Further generators were later installed, the largest of which was 500kW. Coal was delivered there by horse and cart: the coal then cost just three shillings and sixpence (17.5p) per ton.

NESCo, the Newcastle upon Tyne Electric Supply Company, was incorporated in 1889. By 1890 it was supplying electricity from its Pandon Dene power station on the east side of the city. Newcastle, in fact, had two supply companies with the

Charles Merz and others at NESCo saw that there was little future in small-scale operations. They also saw the potential for capturing the growing shipbuilding and engineering industry of Tyneside for electricity. Merz was also consulting engineer to the Walker and Wallsend Company: in 1899 he planned a power station at Neptune Bank, Wallsend, with William McLellan and RP Sloan. Neptune Bank was acquired by NESCo in 1901.

NESCo now became the first electricity generator in the country to supply three-phase electricity operating at a pressure of 5,500 volts - a form of power best suited to industrial applications, whilst lower voltages could be supplied to domestic customers.

Neptune Bank was regarded not just as the fount of electric power supply in Tyneside but also as 'the beginning of the era of electric power utilisation all over the kingdom'. It originally contained four 700kW alternators; these were later augmented by two 1500kW alternators driven by steam turbines made by Parsons; they were the largest of their kind in the world, and operated so successfully that Cunard was persuaded to go for propulsion machinery of the same type for The Mauritania.

Top left: W Farrel on duty at Dunston 'A' Power Station in 1931. *Left:* A linesman perched high above Newcastle. *Above right:* A map of the area in which the Company was authorised to supply electricity.

A new power station opened at Carville in 1904 which supplied both collieries and the North Eastern Railway for the electrification of the track between Newcastle and Tynemouth. It also supplied power via the High Level Bridge to Gateshead and to the north east of County Durham via a cable tunnel from Carville to Hebburn, a tunnel constructed at a depth of 120 feet which was 1,000 feet long and six feet in diameter.

Carville was a landmark in power station design and secured the reputation of the Newcastle based consultants and designers Merz and McLellan. It was the largest public supply station in Europe, and the first of any size to be powered by Parsons' steam turbines, ten times the average size then being installed across Britain.

In 1906 NESCo became the first undertaking to adopt the balanced electrical protection gear of the Merz-Price system, which significantly improved reliability. That same year NESCo also became the first to use 'metal-clad'

switchgear in its substations, a decision which would bring to Tyneside the important switchgear industry of which Reyrolle and Company would become central.

NESCo installed the first such switchgear at the Swan Hunter yard. NESCo had extended its operations by building a transmission system of underground cables and overhead power lines, at first using 6kV. Also in 1906 the company became the first to introduce 20kV transmission, an improvement which minimised power losses over long distances.

Meanwhile, DISCo remained a separate lighting enterprise, whilst at the same time several local authorities in the region operated their own municipal lighting stations which also sold power to industry. The Newcastle Corporation used its power station at Manors to power the tramways; Middlesbrough and Tynemouth, however, took their supplies from companies in the NESCo group. In 1889 NESCo had supplied electricity for lighting within an area of just 11 square miles; by 1914 the system covered 1,400 square miles. By then the conversion to three-phase 40 Hz AC was well under way and was to be the key to large scale interconnected operation, the largest integrated power system in Europe at the time, and making possible the creation of large central generators.

Top left: Carliol House, company head office until 2003. *Bottom left:* An electricity showroom at Carliol House in the 1930s. *Left and below:* Two of the company's many showrooms. *Above:* A 2000 volt/220 volt kiosk type substation.

Economies of scale benefited everyone. In 1899 the cost of electricity per unit had been four pence; by 1905 the cost was just a fraction over one penny per unit. In the first decade of the 20th century sales increased by a factor of 30, far in excess of growth elsewhere; the load factor now averaged 45 per cent compared to little more than 20 per cent in other areas of the country.

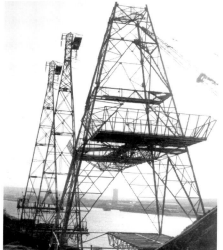

Another local first was the principle of centralised control: displaying, controlling and operating the high voltage network from a central control room. The first system control room was in Carville. The control diagram took up 960 square feet and displayed the generating stations, substations and transmission and distribution network; it was run with the help of the company's own private telephone system.

After the First World War ended in 1918 demand rose steeply, and in 1924 NESCo was the first electricity authority in the country to adopt 66,000 volts (66kV) for transmission purposes. High voltage lines were run between the Tees and the Tyne, and north to Bedlington in the Northumberland coalfield. In built up areas the company became the first to make commercial use of underground cable operating at 66kV. When the Government set the scene for establishing the national grid it was NESCo which provided the model for that grid.

Even during the economic depression of the 1920s demand for electricity continued to grow. Carliol House, completed between 1924 and 1927, was built as NESCo's new headquarters and would remain as the headquarters of Northern Electric until 2003. Carliol House was Newcastle's first important modern office building in the modernised classical style of the inter-war period. The building incorporated many technical innovations introduced by the architect L Couves of Newcastle. An innovative heating system used 60 tons of electrically-heated water circulating through coiled pipes in the ceilings, whilst it was one of the first buildings in the world to incorporate an integral vacuum cleaning system in which cleaners were plugged straight into the walls. The high-speed electric lifts too were considered to be the most up-to-date in the country, travelling at 430 feet per minute. The building also incorporated a luxury cinema and lecture theatre with seating for 70, used to educate consumers by means of lectures and demonstrations. Faced with Portland stone rather than Newcastle's traditional sandstone, the grandeur of the exterior continued inside with the wide use of marble and mahogany. The mixture of Art Deco and stripped classicism with a distinct Egyptian flavour was a popular feature of many buildings of the period.

In the meantime the use of electricity in the home was beginning to make life easier and more enjoyable for everyone, not least housewives: after electric lights had come irons, heaters and fans, followed by cookers, washing machines and fridges. The growth in the use of electrical appliances in the home was actively promoted by NESCo through its shops and mobile showrooms. As a result, throughout the 1930s and beyond, the number of connected customers in the city and the amount of electricity they used grew dramatically.

Top left: *The control room in the 1950s.* **Centre:** *Electricity pylons being erected in 1983.* **Below:** *The board visiting a meter station in 1985.*

Use of electricity in the countryside was boosted in 1934 when the Royal Agricultural Society's show was held in Newcastle. Lower electricity distribution costs heralded a drive towards rural electrification which, after a pause from 1939-45, resumed after the second world war and would eventually be completed in the 1950s and 1960s. The post-war drive to expand the electrical network was extremely successful. By 1952 around 80 per cent of rural premises were receiving supplies, though the balance of farms and other rural communities had to wait for up to ten years more to be connected.

At the same time NEEB was concerned to standardise distribution voltages which varied throughout the area, and to standardise prices so that all its domestic customers paid the same rates. A great expansion of the network after the Second World War increased the number of staff working for the newly created NEEB to a peak of 9,000 in 1965 (increasing efficiency would see that number fall to 3,500 by the end of the century).

Immediately after the war the NEEB's largest customer was the coal industry which took as much electricity as all the other domestic and commercial customers put together. Today, with the coal industry in the North East restricted to a number of opencast sites, demand is much more evenly distributed between domestic customers and industry.

Meanwhile, throughout the 1950s and 1960s price increases to customers were below the rate of inflation, despite the cost of developing the network, and there was a significant growth in off-peak electricity available more cheaply at night. All this changed, however, from the early 1970s when the twin shocks of miners' strikes and the Middle East Oil Crisis made electricity more expensive to produce and distribute: prices rose accordingly. Suddenly energy conservation was on the agenda and the days of 10 per cent annual growth were at an end. Over the next twenty years, prices would fall again, quite dramatically in some cases, and customers of Northern Electric saw smaller bills, better service and rising investment in a company which paid a strong and positive role in the local community.

Northern Electric was bought in 1996 by CalEnergy, since renamed MidAmerican Energy Holdings Company. Two years later the company began selling both electricity and gas; it was the first company to offer such a dual package. More change soon followed. Northern Electric now sold its power supply

business to Innogy in return for the electricity distribution business of Yorkshire Electricity. Northern Electric's main focus would now be on delivering electricity throughout almost 100,000 km of cable to over 3.6 million customers. Northern Electric's retail appliance business was sold to its managers in 2002.

In 2003, after 76 years, Northern Electric said goodbye to its historic headquarters in Newcastle's Carliol House and moved its head office to a new building in Grey Street. Today, with sites throughout the area and its customer contact centre based at Penshaw, Northern Powergrid remains just as committed as its predecessors to its customers and the region.

Since October 2011, the company's name has been Northern Powergrid. That completed the consolidation of the two businesses, Northern Electric Distribution and Yorkshire Electricity Distribution, which had already been run as a single business since the merger in 2001.The company is now facing the biggest challenges to its operations for many years as a result of the battle against climate change. The trend towards smaller scale electricity generation means much more generation connected directly to the network (20,000 houses in the NE alone now have solar panels on their roof). And the North East is leading the way creating the charging infrastructure for electric vehicles.

Northern Powergrid is also leading the country's largest smart grid project, the Customer-Led Network Revolution. In 2010 a £54 million project, with local partners Durham and Newcastle Universities, and Newcastle-based fuel poverty campaigner National Energy Action, was launched, investigating ways to accommodate these changes while keeping costs to customers down.

Though back in its early days the future of the electricity industry may have been unpredictable, one thing we can say today with perfect certainty is that one way or another electricity is here for good.

Facing page, top and below: Northern Powergrid technicians at work. **Left:** Northern Powergrid's network which extends from north Northumberland, south to the Humber and northern Lincolnshire, and from the east coast to the Pennines.

Morpeth
Newcastle
Sunderland
Durham
Darlington
Middlesbrough
NORTHEAST
Scarborough
Bridlington
York
Bradford   Leeds
YORKSHIRE   Hull
Huddersfield
Scunthorpe
Doncaster   Grimsby
Sheffield

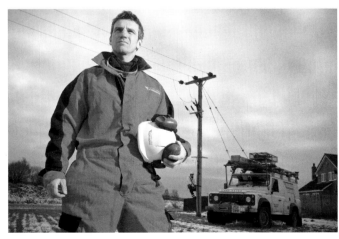

MKW Engineering Ltd
Skilled at Solutions

Gazelle Wind Turbines is the newest company in the MKW Engineering family and was formed in 1998 in response to an opportunity to produce small to medium-sized wind turbines for the UK and other markets.

MKW Engineering Limited was established in 1976 by the Founding Director Mr Vincent Wright who had many years' experience in the design and build of special-purpose machinery.

In 1977 a small industrial unit, which had previously been coal mining colliery buildings, was leased and manufacturing started.

By 1980 a small number of regular clients had been established, more machine tools purchased, and a local workforce of seven skilled operators was being employed.

It became clear at that time that a niche market existed for specialist engineering solutions to manufacturing problems experienced by clients.

It was also clear that the leased buildings had served their purpose and were no longer suitable for the type of work being undertaken. During 1980 land was bought at Stargate, which was also a former colliery. There the company now designed and built a special-purpose unit complete with overhead crane.

The MKW Group has responded to the challenges facing industry in the early 21st century to become an innovative leader in the provision of engineering solutions.

At MKW, there are no problems in engineering: only challenges and solutions. That's because of the MKW Group's across-the-board engineering capability - from design, to manufacture, testing and installation, as well as maintenance and project management.

The MKW Group is an association of four companies, all based at Stargate Business Park, Ryton, Gateshead. Together they employ some 150 people, boasting a turnover of close to £8 million.

Since it was established in the 1970s MKW has built an extensive blue chip client base across the sub-sea, defence and other sectors. It has invested heavily in cutting edge technology to ensure it can deliver high quality bespoke solutions to specific customer challenges.

Total Maintenance and Engineering Ltd (TME) was set up in 1995 to provide an engineering maintenance and installation service to complement MKW Engineering.

Stargate Precision Engineering Ltd (SPE) specialises in the production of precision-machined components for the aerospace, sub-sea and pharmaceutical industries. That company was also established in 1995.

The focus of the company now became directed towards project engineering, requiring not only the factory facilities, but also that of skilled staff. As a result of this, more engineering personnel capable of tackling projects from small assemblies to large integrated projects were employed.

The following years demonstrated the success of that strategy, with rapid growth occurring. In order to accommodate that increase in demand the facilities at Stargate were expanded in several stages to the present 90,000 sq. feet factory and 20,000 sq. ft. of office space.

Both the engineering facilities and the factory machinery were increased to allow larger projects to be undertaken, and be manufactured in-house with the benefit in both quality and project coordination. Engineering capability had by then been developed so that all engineering disciplines were represented within the company.

During the late 1980s and into the 1990s changes in the region resulting from the decline of the shipbuilding and mining industries were, happily, not reflected in a similar downturn for MKW Engineering. The company took change as an opportunity to expand into the new markets which began to replace the older traditional ones.Process Plant, Electrical Generation, TV Manufacture, Car Manufacturing, Medical Equipment and Defence Equipment now became the new spheres of business for the company.

Starting with early prototypes of Radiology Treatment Equipment brought MKW into a new realm of high precision manufacturing, with complex, very accurate, and medical industry compliant, machinery having to be developed to cater for clients' requirements. These new demands required additional machining: large computer-controlled equipment was purchased in order to guarantee accuracy and continuity of precision equipment.

To underpin these developments ISO 9001 quality systems (then BS5750) were introduced, and in 1988 MKW celebrated being one of the first North East companies to become accredited with this international standard of quality achievement.

Additional investments in machinery and facilities to cater for the demands from the new markets created in turn the need to set up additional facilities; these were completed in 1995 with the formation of Stargate Precision Engineering covering small-medium volume precision machining, and Total Maintenance and Engineering which now handled the MKW Engineering support and maintenance business.

*Top left, facing page: Group Managing Director, Michael Wright. **Bottom, facing page:** At work in the Large Machining and Inspection department. **Above:** A nuclear capping plate manufactured by MKW.*

Additional market opportunities were now discovered in the areas of Defence and Aerospace, Oil & Gas and Subsea Engineering.

Today MKWs products are in use all over the world in. Medical Equipment includes patient radiotherapy equipment and nuclear medicine. Naval and Ground Based Satellite Communications Antennas are used by the navies of Great Britain, Spain, Germany, Portugal, Italy, Turkey, Canada, USA, Australia, UAE and others, with over 380 systems shipped in the past 10 years.

Oil & Gas components for subsea, topside and vessel operations are a major source of contracts. Hydraulic Systems are in use in many industries including Oil & Gas Exploration and Production, Chemical and Process Industries, Fuel Transfer Systems, Drilling and Handling Industries, Paint Manufacture and Process Environments. Renewable Energy – Turbine Installation ad Power Integration, Offshore Turbine Access and Maintenance.

The company has been a continuous supporter of training for new staff and apprentices as a way to introduce people to engineering; a comprehensive training period results in qualified engineers and skilled personnel. At any one time there are between 4 and 6 apprentices going through training. Whilst some leave and move to pastures new once their

apprenticeship is complete, many stay with the company and move up the organisation; indeed two current company directors served their apprenticeships at MKW Engineering.

MKW Engineering Ltd has responded to far-reaching changes to the UK engineering sector to become an innovative leader in the provision of engineering solutions. This means that MKW can provide customised solutions to individual engineering challenges, and manage the entire process from design, manufacture, assembly and installation, all from one site.

Typically, MKW's design team creates bespoke solutions in response to client inquiries. These can range from design work on specialist machinery, to process equipment, product redesign, production, and project management.

Although MKW does not take any of its own products to market, it does nonetheless frequently produce products for clients in significant quantities. These include sophisticated components for the defence, medical and sub-sea sectors.

MKW, with a £5 million turnover, has invested heavily in state-of-the-art machinery, including the first five-axis vertical machining centre of its kind in the UK. Other on-site capabilities include assembly, fabrication, inspection and welding of carbon

steels, aluminium and stainless steel, sheet metal working and painting.

The company's 100-strong workforce prides itself on core skills, such as welding, machining, working to short lead times, or finding manufacturing solutions to complex specifications.

Among the on-site specialist facilities are a Clean Assembly area for fitting, for example, electrical wiring components, and testing products such as medical and defence equipment. The fully equipped paint shop boasts an extensive range of key industrial capabilities.

Gazelle Wind Turbines Ltd was established in 1998, when The MKW Group responded to research by the North Energy Associates, specialists in renewable energy, which indicated a market niche for small to medium size wind turbines. A prototype machine was completed with assistance from a Department of Trade and Industry SMART grant.

The Gazelle provides an elegant power solution for medium-sized users, such as schools, small businesses, rural companies, water works and eco-centres. Its 11m carbon fibre epoxy rotor generates 20kW of electricity, offering scope for

users to supply energy back to the National Grid and offset charges for power.

Gazelle was initially run by Dr Garry Jenkins, a founding director of North Energy Associates, who brought his considerable experience in wind energy to the business. Under new Managing Director Ken Chaplin, Gazelle is now well positioned for further growth in this vibrant sector.

Stargate Precision Engineering Ltd (SPE) uses the latest CNC (computer numerically controlled) equipment to manufacture precision-machined components for a range of engineering disciplines, including: Defence, Sub-sea and offshore, Petrochemical, Electrical generation and transmission, Oil and gas, Machinery manufacturers, and Process industries.

The company was spun off from MKW Engineering Ltd in 1995 in response to the requirement for a reliable supplier of complex medical and other precision components within The MKW Group.

By 2004 Stargate boasted a 20-strong skilled workforce, turning over some £0.75 million.

Stargate has continued to invest in the highest quality and performance CNC equipment and inspection facilities to create one of the most capable machine shops in the North of England.

CNC turning and milling now covers up to five axes, and the facility to convert drawings in electronic format to machining programmes ensures minimal delay in fulfilling orders.

Total Maintenance and Engineering Ltd (TME) was originally formed in July 1995 as a member of the MKW Group to carry out on-site installations.

Top, facing page: Five-axis machining. *Bottom, facing page: Subsea assembly. Above left and below:* A Gazelle Wind Turbine manufactured at the MKW facility pictured below.

Since then, TME has expanded its operations to provide a full project planning and installation service, while its 1,000 sq metre workshop, equipped with three ten-tonne overhead cranes, enables fabrication and heavy equipment overhauls on-site.

TME operates a rigorous health and safety policy and in 2003 earned the SAFEcontractor accreditation.

Today, TME's workforce of 40-plus mechanical, electrical and fabrication engineers carries out tasks ranging from ship maintenance for the defence sector, to equipment overhaul for major blue chip clients. With a core customer base of about 30, TME now has a £2 million turnover.

The MKW Group's innovative approach to engineering extends to the way it trains and develops its people, with the most innovative feature being the Group's, possibly unique, International Journeyman apprentice training programme.

Under International Journeyman, locally recruited trainees serve two years of their apprenticeship in France, where they acquire a language skill, as well as a very solid engineering grounding.

The scheme is a reflection of the MKW Group's commitment to assuring the future of quality engineering in the North East of England. It works in partnership with the Regional Technology Centre, Sunderland (RTC North) and Les Compagnons du Devoir, in France, to ensure young apprentices from the region can enjoy a first class training at MKW and in France - and go out into the world of engineering with a new language as well as engineering skills.

So positive has been The MKW Group's experience with its French training 'journey' that it is now driving efforts to try and emulate aspects of the French model in the North East. MKW has been in talks with parties including ONE NorthEast, Tyneside Learning & Skills Council and Gateshead Council, with the aim of taking the initiative forward together. The MKW Group sees the French method as placing a much-needed greater emphasis on acquiring practical skills in the workplace.

Michael K Wright, Chief Executive, is also a Director of Training & Development Resources Ltd (TDR), the Tyneside-based Learning and Skills Council-funded apprentice training company.

The Group has been instrumental in the introduction of pioneering ventures in apprentice training, including Student Apprenticeships and Tomorrow's Engineers. With International Journeyman, these schemes offer students a much wider range of options than formerly and give companies more cost-effective training solutions.

The MKW Group's purpose-built Training Centre provides the location for a variety of training courses and initiatives. As the following list demonstrates, these include a number of partnership and community involvements, all geared to help ensure that the North East can provide the engineering skills it needs to ensure the ongoing prosperity of the sector and its contribution to the wider economy. The courses include: Tomorrow's Engineers Programme, Further education for Apprentices, All in-house training, including manual handling, Pendant Crane use etcetera, Investors in People - Best practice visits, Durham University Business School MSc modular visit programme, Regional Technology Centre - Best practice visits, Basic Skills courses, Astrium (EADS) Space school programme. This is the first time this programme has been run externally by EADS Astrium, one of MKW's key trading partners.

In February 2012 HRH Prince Andrew Duke of York visited MKW Engineering to see for himself the company's training arrangements, and the new technologies that were, and still are, being developed.

Most recently MKW Engineering gave support to the Bluebird Project which undertook to rebuild/restore to its former glory the Bluebird high speed boat which was raised from the waters of Lake Coniston following the tragic speed record attempt in January 1967 by Donald Campbell. The project involved taking the original blueprints of the water-planing shoes and using modern 3D design techniques. In 2013, using machine-programming, the company was able to produce complex components identical to the ones lost in 1967.

Facing page: Training with the MKW at the Group's purpose-built Training Centre. **Facing page bottom:** *MKW offices.* **Above:** *HRH Prince Andrew Duke of York's visit to MKW Engineering.* **Below:** *At work on the Bluebird project using 3D design software.*

White Bros. Ltd
Quality Stainless Steel Fabrication

White Bros (Newcastle on Tyne) Ltd, today based on the Gosforth Industrial Estate, is a manufacturer of high quality stainless steel fabrications and a provider of site servicing, pipework, coded welding and metrology services.

For some 130 years the firm has been developing the skills and experience which enable it to provide exceptional quality, service, and a 'can do' attitude. Customers are from a wide range of industries, including food, pharmaceutical, nuclear, bio-tech, semiconductor, oil and gas. The company's fabrications are used by manufacturers across the world.

For the best part of the 20th century the company operated first from Fife Street and then from Westgate Road and Corporation Street.

The firm was established in 1884; its founders were not surprisingly, two brothers - George and Ernest White. A third, and much younger brother, Alan, born in 1900, joined the firm later and continued to work in the business right up until his death in 1972. The business was originally established to provide the farming community in Northumberland and Durham with dairy equipment, plumbing and electrical installations.

For 60 years the firm occupied 236, Westgate Road, together with the stable block to the rear (in Corporation Street) from where the firm only moved in 1989. There were five children in the White family: two girls, Olive and Grace, occupied the spare accommodation in the front terrace in Westgate Road until they passed away in the late 1960s.

By the 1920s the White brothers were manufacturing their own products, such as milk churns and separators, whilst also making and selling such, now barely-remembered items, such as hand-bells for milkmen to ring in the street, and leather cash bags for them to keep their takings in.

Top: Whites working on a farm on Kenton Lane in the mid 1950s. The backdrop is towards Newcastle Airport. The building to the left of the hayrick is still standing. *Left:* Early White Bros products.

In the 1950s the company moved into producing stainless steel equipment for the ice cream industry. Alan White in the latter part of his life moved the company more into the industrial side of the business, believing, rightly, that this was where the future of the company lay.

It was, however, Thomas Lowther who had joined the company in 1936 at the age of 20 as a cost clerk who further developed the company in the industrial sector, eventually completing the move totally away from farming and into sheet metal.

Thomas Lowther was destined to eventually become Managing Director and finally the owner of White Bros following Alan White's death. Tom Lowther remained very active in the company until 1989.

Since the Second World War two generations have grown up who have no recollection that doorstep deliveries of milk did not always come in a milk bottle with a foil top. Fewer and fewer people now remember that once upon a time the milkman often came around wheeling a milk churn on a handcart.

Back then the milkman rang a hand-bell to attract housewives who came out of their homes carrying a jug into which the milk would be poured. Given the many odd-sized pots and jugs which appeared, how did the housewife know she was getting a full pint?

With the assistance of the firm's current Chairman and owner Peter Harding, Tom eventually moved the company to its present premises at Gosforth Industrial Estate. The old premises had been very dilapidated and operations had to be carried out on different floors and levels as the site sloped steeply.

Top: The old factory factory at 67 Corporation Street. *Centre:* Tom Lowther who ran the company for 40 years. *Below:* Westgate Road in April 1989.

Older readers will remember that the milkman had a variety of different sized ladles - a gill, half a pint, a pint and a quart - each bearing a government weights and measures stamp. The ladles could then be dipped into his churn to serve a standard portion. The milkman needed to buy his stamped imperial milk measures from somewhere, and in this part of the world the supplier was White Brothers who could provide ladles of up to a gallon capacity, and measuring pails of up to four gallons along with tripod and scales to measure and weigh milk in the dairy.

A copy of the company's 1923 catalogue lists many such hardware items for the dairy, it also, however, lists such items as pumps and hydraulic rams, portable farm engines and electric light installations.

What limited space existed was fragmented so that flow-line production was impossible and the effective manufacturing space was inadequate for the growing and increasingly diversified workload. To add to the firm's problems access both to the site, and within it, was extremely difficult

Peter Harding's plans involved investment in modern machine and technology, investments, which resulted in White Bros becoming the leading stainless steel sheet metal workers in the area.

The company now has state-of-the-art computerised Radan CAD/CAM Amada CNC shear, pressbrakes, laser and punching machines. The company takes particular pride in its ISO 9000 quality approval, Health & Safety and environmental policy.

The site increased in size in 1994 and 1998 by the acquisition of adjacent premises to cope with increasing demand. A new polishing shop was created with dust extraction booths and a great deal of effort went into noise and vibration control. A new polishing machine was introduced in 2000 which combined increased speed of production coupled with health and safely improvements.

Other innovations had taken place throughout the 1990s. In 1995 White Bros introduced its first standard product since the days of its catalogues for the farming community. Liquisafe, as its name implies, is a safe method of transferring chemicals between containers rather than the conventional dip tube method. In 1997 White Bros acquired Stellex Ltd with a factory and offices based at Hadston in Morpeth, Northumberland. Stellex was a catering equipment manufacturer in stainless steel and other materials. The business was an ideal addition giving White Bros a major product line of its own which fitted well with its computer-aided modern machinery.

During the recession in the years following the financial crisis of 2008 Whites, like many other businesses suffered a downturn in trade and was forced to consolidate and concentrate on its core business. A strategic review was performed which identified areas of improvement. Shop floor workflow

Today, in the 21st century, equally unaware, thousands more will have regular contact with the firm, buying food which has been processed in plants furnished with the firm's equipment or eating in canteens and restaurants which have been outfitted using White Brothers' stainless steel fittings.

The story of the business, as much as that of individuals and families, has been one with many twists and unexpected turns. No doubt the future will have just as many surprises in store – but whatever those challenges may be White Bros (Newcastle on Tyne) Ltd intends to rise to the top, as it always has – just like cream in a milk jug.

management has been improved and initiatives started to increase sales.

White Bros co-founded Continuous Retorts Ltd in 2009, a business which is now designing and developing a highly innovative new cooking process for various food sectors.

In 2012, Greggs the Bakers moved off the industrial estate which provided White Bros the opportunity to buy another adjoining property. This provided an extra 6,500 sq ft of space and the capacity. As a sign of this increased post-recession confidence the company has undergone a re-branding exercise to refresh its public image.

The company currently employ a total of 48 staff. Skilled labour can, however, be difficult to find, particularly for a firm like White Bros that needs employees with a depth and breadth of experience and skill that is uncommon. The company finds that the best employees are those who have trained within it. The company has a very low turnover of staff and most of their skilled staff are White Bros trained.

Every year the firm takes on at least two apprentices who are put through a training course with Rolls Royce (formerly Vickers Training). White Bros now believes that with the assistance of Rolls Royce training it has one of, if not the best quality sheet metal apprenticeship schemes on Tyneside.

The business specialises in stainless steel, highly finished, quality sheet metal fabrications, mainly for the food and pharmaceutical industries. Customers are to be found all over the UK rather than just the local area. Some products are exported to Europe, America and Asia.

Throughout the 20th century thousands of Newcastle residents would unknowingly have had daily contact with White Brother's products as their wives and mothers collected milk poured into their jugs using the firm's ladles.

Facing page top: White Bros' premises in 2000. Facing page centre, bottom, and above pictures: White Bros have years of experience making high quality bespoke fabrications of all degrees of complexity for a wide range of applications. Platforms, skids, vessels, conveyors, hoppers, ducts, chutes, isolators/glove boxes, street furniture, building signage, public art, often to very demanding quality specifications. Whatever the requirement the firm can produce an effective solution. Below, from left: Directors, Gavin Wragby, Peter Harding and Steve Roberts.

Wingrove Motor Company Ltd
Five Generations of Motoring

The Wingrove Motor Co Ltd, is a family business founded on the main western artery leading into in the heart of Newcastle in August 1925, by John Myers Dalkin Snr, a local cattle auctioneer, and the major financial backer, along with other family members.

Those were the days of mudguards and running boards, semaphore indicators and real leather upholstery - and when colour and style meant a choice of black or black!

Cars and motor sport have long been in the family blood, and the founder's son, John Myers Dalkin, Jnr, known as 'Jack', was soon part of the company, which he had joined in 1927, as well as part of the local motorcycle racing scene. Jack developed a love for motor sports, joining both the Newcastle and District Motor Club and the Northumbria Motor Club.

Then came WWII, with heavy bombing in the area due to Newcastle's industrial shipbuilding and ammunitions production. Inevitably, war caused a halt to further progress by the company. Not least of the problems, for both the firm and its customers, was petrol rationing. Post-war petrol rationing provided its own problems. Nevertheless, the business continued to weather such storms, and emerged in the 1950s ready to meet the challenges and opportunities which the 1950s would bring.

For the Dalkin family the post-war years also brought two sons, Brian and Peter.

Motor bikes were swapped for cars and in 1954 and 1955 Jack, now the firm's Managing Director, took part in the famous Monte Carlo Rally, as well as refurbishing the West Road Garage.

Top: Wingrove's, West Road premises in the 1920s. *Above:* A bus from the 1970s carrying Wingrove advertising. *Left:* West Road in the 1960s.

By 1962, both sons had joined the company; Peter had by then completed his motor mechanic apprenticeship and had started tuning high performance cars, which was his main passion establishing the Perdal Performance Centre. Peter became responsible for an offshoot of the Wingrove Motor Company, Perdal Developments. Making cars go faster was grist to Peter's personal mill, and he found himself receiving letters and requests from all over the world which ranged from two-shilling components to fully-tuned engines which sold for around £620. By the late 1960s, Perdal's had an export turnover of £3,000 a month - and it was still growing

Peter and his wife Eunice's three children, Louise (1963), Lindsay (1965), and Elliott (1966), were all born hearing the noise and excitement of their father preparing engines and racing Clubmans around the UK, along with listening to stories from their grandfather about his racing exploits.

The business grew and grew from its beginning as a repair garage with petrol sales. In 1966, it became an agent for Standard Triumph, by which time space was becoming cramped at the West Road and a new larger workshop was acquired a mile away on Elswick Road. This provided new workshop space and plenty of room for Perdal to expand. With backing by Shell and BP for a self-service filling station it meant there was room to

further redevelop the West Road site. In 1969, Citroen Cars Limited appointed the Wingrove Motor Company as its distributor and service agent for Northumberland and Durham.

During the 1970s, Wingrove was a prominent part of the North East motoring scene, with local motor show events, sponsorship in the local press, and not forgetting the motorsport!

'Jack' Dalkin passed away in 1970 leaving sons Brian and Peter as directors to expand the business. There were new sites in Gateshead and Whitley Bay, both with car sales, workshop and petrol, resulting in increased sales and awareness of Citroen around the north east.

The site on Elswick Road expanded, with the construction of a fully equipped body repair centre, a growing parts department, and the base for Peter's rally team.

Top: Cars filling up at Wingrove in the 1970s. Left: Elswick Road Workshops, also home to Perdal Developments. Pictured are Keith Bowmaker, workshop foreman and racing driver, with Eunice Dalkin, wife of director Peter. Below: The NE Motor Show, The Links, Whitley Bay. Wingrove were a regular exhibitor with the whole garage being involved throughout the 1970s.

Peter, like his father before him, competed in several RAC rallies and other major UK rallies. Originally a Citroen DS would be seen thundering through the forests, later to be replaced by the more agile GS cars. There were also a very exciting few years of 2CV Cross in which Wingrove fielded a team of several staff member at various events around the UK and Europe in their team bus.

Staying on a competitive theme the 1980s started with Peter taking part in the 2nd Paris Dakar Rally. The decade also saw the resignation of Brian Dalkin, and subsequent share reallocation, with Peter's wife Eunice becoming a director. During the decade another expansion took place at Elswick, with a large purpose-built showroom and offices erected (designed by architect daughter Louise) whilst sons Lindsay and Elliott became part of the business. Lindsay worked at the newly acquired Hexham garage, and Elliott joining Perdal and the

tuning and motor sport element of the firm, as well as competing with his father and other members of staff in auto cross, rally cross and grass track in the competitive Visa, LN and Saxo, at both local and national events. By now Wingrove was also a major Webber Carburettor agent.

In the 1990s, along with Citroen's changing product range, came new challenges; corporate ID meant a new look for all the sites. A lot of hard work and commitment saw Wingrove regularly amongst the top three dealer in the UK, with sales topping 1,000 vehicles each year; the parts department had the largest dealer stock of Citroen parts in the UK. With that success within the dealer network Peter found himself as Chairman of the Citroen UK Dealer Council for several years.

By the end of the century the company's property portfolio had been consolidated. The original West Road garage was sold with the main base now at Elswick Road. The retail motor trade was changing, and Wingrove took up the opportunity at the beginning of the new millennium to become one of the first motor dealerships on Silverlink Motor Retail Park in Wallsend, Newcastle.

The company also acquired a garage on the West Road, nearer to the newly rerouted A1, which led to the subsequent in-house construction of a new showroom in 2002.

Elswick Road and Whitley Bay branches were now sold on, the bodyshop relocated into a new state-of-the-art facility in Cramlington, Northumberland, whilst the Silverlink site was refurbished in 2008 as the motor trade side of the development grew.

Sadly, Eunice passed away in 2002 and Peter took partial retirement. He then remarried in 2009 to his now wife Joselyn who is very supportive of all his ventures and the family business.

Top left: Gosforth Park Hotel and the launch of the GS in 1972. Above circled: Peter and Louise Dalkin at the launch party of the Citroen 2CV Charleston, mid-1970s. Left: Peter Dalkin and his trusty 2CV pictured outside Elswick Road after a successful season of national and international 2CV Cross, early 1980s. Above: Peter Dalkin with Citroen UK Rally team at new Elswick Rd showroom, 1990s.

Families being families, Lindsay left in 2011, and his sister Louise is now getting to grips with the ever-changing role of the business, as a director with her father Peter. Sales margins are getting tighter, but Wingrove is still averaging a £22million annual turnover; the long-standing loyal customer base benefiting from a professional, friendly and reliably after sales team that complements the sales team.

In an ever-changing retail market Wingrove, in partnership with The MetroCentre, Gateshead, Europe's largest shopping centre, has had a continuous nine-month promotion with vehicles and staff inside the main shopping mall, including two very different 'pop up shops', and also made an appearance on BBC3's reality show Shoplife.

Along with the staff from various departments the firm is pleased to be able to say that within the company there are over 800 years of Wingrove service and experience amongst the 75 strong staff, over 40% being at Wingrove for 10 years or more and over 10% in excess of 20 years.

Friendly and loyal staff help give customers confidence, and despite the economic recession Wingrove is still here in the North East, pleased to offer customers a total package: new and used sales, after sales, MOT, service contract, financial advice, courtesy vehicles, full accident damage repair, parts and accessories, and not forgetting care and attention to detail.

Top: Wingrove's sales team at the Metro Centre. **Left:** *Wingrove West, West Road. The new showroom located just one mile down from the original site.* **Below:** *Three generations of family at Wingrove, l-r: Josh Parker (marketing & IT), Peter Dalkin (Director) and Louise Parker (Director).*

After being Citroen Dealers for almost half a century Wingrove is looking to offer their customers a wider choice. With the formation of 'The Motor Company NE' in November 2012 the company has taken on Great Wall 4x4 pickups, launched at the Chinese New Year Celebrations in Newcastle's own China Town. A new franchise has meant the company is once again becoming a regular exhibitor at the local county and agricultural shows.

The firm has recently taken on Subaru and Isuzu, and is currently constructing a separate showroom at the West Road garage to accommodate non-Citroen franchise vehicles.

Wingrove remains unquestionably a family business. Peter is still at the helm, with son, daughter, son-in-law, and now a grandson representing the 5th generation of the family, all involved.

Grainger plc
Investing in Homes since 1912

Celebrating its 100th birthday in 2012 Grainger plc, based in Citygate, Newcastle, is the UK's largest listed specialist residential landlord and property manager. The company's objective is to be a leader in the residential market, delivering sustainable long-term returns to its investors and partners from a combination of sales, rents and fee income. Grainger's strategy and business reflect the changing dynamics of the residential market. The company uses its core skills (trading, managing, investing, developing and fund management) and its agility to take advantage of the opportunities presented by these changes in the housing market. At the end of September 2013, Grainger had approximately £2.8bn of residential assets under management across the UK and Germany.

Today, Grainger is a FTSE 250 business on the London Stock Exchange. In 2012 Grainger won Best Property Company –

Residential at the Estates Gazette Awards, and Asset Manager of the Year at the RESI Awards in both 2012 and 2013.

Established in Newcastle Upon Tyne in 1912 as The Grainger Trust, the company was launched to acquire and manage controlled and assured residential tenancies.

Now the company delivers strong returns from its reversionary and market rented assets, and its residential expertise allows it to supplement these returns by generating management fee income.

The firm was founded by members of the Dickinson and Storey families, who were solicitors and surveyors respectively. Their names continue in Bond Dickinson solicitors and Storeys Edmund Symonds surveyors. Although the Storey family connection was severed in the 1930s, the Dickinson family remained heavily involved until very recently. The firm was chaired from the sixties through to the early nineties by Ian Dickinson and then by Robert Dickinson. His cousins, Stephen and Rupert, separately acted as Chief

Top: *Where it all began, Cross House on the junction Fenkle Street and Westgate Road, Newcastle.* ***Left:*** *Royal Buildings (far left) and Chaucer Buildings (left), former premises of the firm.* ***Above:*** *Robert Dickinson (left), former Chairman of the Granger Trust Group and Stephen Dickinson, former Managing Director.*

The Grainger Trust changed its name to Grainger plc in 2007, although in November 2012, to mark its centenary, it brought back Grainger Trust as the name for its 'for profit' registered provider of social housing.

Over 100 years Grainger has built up a large portfolio of wholly and co-owned residential properties across the UK and Germany. Grainger's portfolio reflects the diversity of the housing stock in both countries, and through its detailed local knowledge and the ability to invest, trade and manage residential property Grainger is able to deliver best value.

In the UK, Grainger's assets have continued to outperform the general residential market, with an 8.3% increase in values in the year to the end of September 2013 compared to Nationwide and Halifax house price indices with an average increase of 5.6%.

Grainger's largest source of income is through the sale of properties. Every year Grainger sells around 600 properties when they become vacant, and occasionally sells further properties while they are tenanted when they no longer present sufficient value growth prospects. This income stream is primarily driven by Grainger's large portfolio of reversionary assets. The company acquires tenanted properties at a discount to vacant possession value and sells them when they become vacant. Historically, the majority of these reversionary assets were what are referred to as 'regulated tenancies', however these type of tenancies have not been created since a change in legislation in 1989.

Top left: Citygate, St James' Boulevard, Newcastle, head office of Grainger plc. **Above left:** *Chief Executive, Andrew Cunningham.* **Below:** *Grainger plc's Dibdin House, North London, property.*

Executive, with Rupert stepping down in 2009 when the present incumbent Andrew Cunningham succeeded to the post.

The bulk of Grainger's housing stock came from companies such as British Coal, British Steel and English China Clay. These companies sold their tenanted stock which the Trust bought and managed.

Originally based in Cross House, the Trust stayed there until 1975 when a move was made to new headquarters at Royal Buildings. There was a further move to Chaucer Buildings, 57 Grainger Street, then to Times Square and finally today's base in Citygate.

Throughout the eighties the Trust continued its growth, entering into land development with the acquisition of 350 acres between Basingstoke and the M3; it later acquired Channel Hotels and Properties which owned over 700 London flats, resulting in its first London office.

In the early 2000's Grainger acquired the Bradford Property Trust plc (BPT), creating the largest quoted residential property portfolio in the UK.

Since 2006 Grainger has developed its German branch, and with the successful procurement of Francono Rhein-Main AG for €41.4m, critical mass in Germany was created, enhancing Grainger's rental income stream through this large market rented portfolio.

In addition to acquiring regulated tenancies, Grainger has supplemented its reversionary portfolio through acquiring home reversion assets which have similar return profiles to regulated tenancies. This part of Grainger's business is now a market leader in the UK equity release sector.

Grainger's retirement solutions business offers home reversion plans with a range of features through Grainger's Bridgewater Equity Release business, which distributes these plans through financial advisers. Grainger is proud to say that it has been voted Best Home Reversion Provider for the past 8 consecutive years.

Grainger's second largest source of income is its rental income. Historically, the types of assets owned provided strong sales income and relatively lower rental income, but as Grainger delivers on its strategy, focusing on the private rented sector, a greater proportion of revenue will come from rents.

The characteristics of the UK housing market are rapidly changing, and there has been and will continue to be a growth within the private rented sector. The UK Government and all major political parties have recognised the importance of the private rented sector and there have been a number of new Government support measures aimed at encouraging its growth.

Grainger has led the way in this space with some notable achievements. For example, Grainger is developing one of the UK's first purpose-built rental blocks in Barking, East London and will rent out and manage the block of 100 flats when it is completed in 2015.

The Royal Borough of Kensington & Chelsea also selected Grainger to develop and manage two innovative housing schemes in a 125 year partnership. Grainger will develop affordable, private for sale and private rented residential accommodation on the public sector land and will fund and manage the delivery of the projects.

Grainger has established itself at the forefront of Government initiatives, particularly in the private rented sector. Grainger has been leading the debate, successfully shaping and influencing Government policy and initiatives; the company has recently been shortlisted for the Government's 'build to rent' fund.

Grainger aims to be the first port of call for any organisation seeking to participate in the residential property market, or requiring a solution to issues facing it in this market.

The ability to manage large residential portfolios allows Grainger to offer its expertise and services in the form of fund, property and asset management to third party clients, providing the PLC with an increasing level of recurring income from fees. This has been seen with a series of co-investment deals in both the UK

This page: A selection of Grainger properties: Wellesley, Aldershot - Cambridge Hospital (top left), Mariners Cottage, South Shields (left) and Walkerville, Firtree Avenue, Newcastle upon Tyne (below).

and Germany, including deals with APG and Heitman, as well as the provision of G-RAMP, an asset management platform to Lloyds Bank, and for a partnership with the Defence Infrastructure Organisation (DIO) of the Ministry of Defence at the Aldershot Urban Extension.

Being a long-term player and aligning its interests to those of its partners, through co-investment or shared reward arrangements, are at the heart of Grainger's values.

Grainger is a co-investor in one of the UK's largest market-let residential investment funds, GRIP, alongside Europe's biggest institutional investor, APG, the Dutch pension fund asset manager. In addition Grainger provides fund management, asset management and property management services to the fund for a fee.

For Lloyds Banking Group and other financial institutions Grainger provides a Residential Asset Management Platform (RAMP) to manage residential buy-to-let portfolios that have entered into administration. In this deal, the first of its kind in the UK, Grainger receives fees based on rent, disposals and shared success fees, fully aligning its interests with those of its partners for any assets placed into the RAMP.

In Germany Grainger has a joint venture with the global real estate investment firm Heitman which owns around 3,000 German rented residential units. The Joint Venture is 75:25 owned by Heitman, on behalf of a global institutional investor, and Grainger, respectively. Grainger acts as the fund manager and asset and property manager.

In Aldershot Grainger has entered a long-term relationship with the Defence Infrastructure Organisation of the Ministry of Defence. This has led to a highly complex project to deliver some 3,850 homes and community facilities on historically important, but surplus, military land to create a thriving community to the benefit of Aldershot whilst delivering the best value for the Ministry of Defence.

For over a century now, from its base in Newcastle, Grainger has been making a major contribution to meeting Britain's housing needs. In the 21st century that ambition remains undiminished.

This page: *More properties from the Grainger portfolio: Temperance House, Great Whittington, Northumberland (left), The Village, Acklington, Northumberland (above) and Wiesbaden Grabenstrasse, Germany.*

Thompsons of Prudhoe
Changing the Face of Tyneside

Ever wondered what happened to the the Mayfair, Killingworth Towers, the Cattle Market, Bath Lane College, the old Gallowgate & Leazes Ends stands at St James' Park? Or Northern Rock Tower, the old Newcastle City Library, Westgate House – once voted one of the Top 10 ugliest buildings in the UK – and the famous 'Get Carter' multi-storey car park?

Look no further than Thompsons of Prudhoe which has more than six decades of experience in the demolition and construction industries, and which in 2013 was also busy pulling down the three 16-storey tower blocks at the Chandless Estate in Gateshead, just over the Tyne Bridge.

The business of W&M Thompson was founded on 1 January, 1948, as a simple husband and wife partnership. It became W&M Thompson Limited in 1952 and as the business developed into a group of companies, it became colloquially known as "Thompsons of Prudhoe". As the business developed further and the separate group companies were put into a formal parent/subsidiary structure in 1995, the parent company was called Thompsons of Prudhoe Ltd.

The company was named after its founders William and Margaret Thompson, though they were known as 'Bill' and 'Madge'. Both were from an agricultural background in Cumbria.

Before starting the business Bill was a farm labourer. He then moved to Lancashire working huge Clydesdale horses pulling barges on the Manchester Ship canal.

The business began by hauling agricultural lime, manure, hay, straw and slag (a beneficial fertiliser by-product from steelworks). To begin with there was just Bill and Madge: staff numbers would however eventually grow to over 250 employees today.

Size 10 shovels and flat-bedded trucks were first used for hauling then unloading the materials Thompsons hauled and supplied. The first truck cost £494 17s 4d in 1947. (By contrast a modern Thompson's truck costs £95,000. The most expensive excavator in the current fleet cost over £325,000 - though Thompsons did at one point own the largest Bulldozer in the UK, a Caterpillar D11 bought for £430,000 back in 1988 for ripping rock in their quarries).

How times have changed. Bill had to travel to London to collect that first vehicle, a 6-ton Dodge Platform wagon registration CHH 492. Back then new vehicles had to be run-in at 20 mph for the first 1,000 miles. No wonder that Bill was stopped by the police on the way home for 'loitering'!

In 1948, the business was based at 151, Manchester Road, Astley. In 1950, it moved to 49, West Road, Prudhoe, and operated from there until the mid-1960s. In 1965, a five-acre site at Priestclose, Prudhoe, became the business' depot. That in turn was outgrown, and in 1987 a purpose-built depot and Head Office were constructed at the Low Prudhoe Industrial Estate from where the business is still run from.

Top: *Founders, William and Margaret Thompson on their wedding day.* ***Left:*** *Bill Thompson as a farm labourer.* ***Above inset:*** *Bill Thompson with a Clydesdale horse pulling a barge on the Manchester Canal.*

Bill and Madge's sons, Billy and John, joined the business full-time as soon as they left school (though both helped in the business long before then). Young Billy Thompson passed his driving test on 6 August, 1956, and the 17-year-old took his first load out that same night, all the way to Inverness. John Thompson left school in 1957 and he too was soon both driving, and working in the office at West Road.

John's son, John Jnr, and his eldest daughter, Helen, joined the business when they left school, and today are Directors of the company with their father.

No account of the history of Thompsons of Prudhoe can be written without acknowledging the contribution and names of John Purvis, John Turnbull, Robbie and Tommy Lowden, Bob Nelson, and Ian Hind.

Although Bill and Madge set up the business and gave it a firm footing, it was Billy and John Thompson who really drove the business through the 1970s, 1980s and 1990s to expand from hauliers and suppliers of agricultural products such as hay, straw and lime to a multi-million pound regional heavyweight in the broad construction and industrial contracting services sector, encompassing demolition, bulk excavation/earthworks, skip hire, waste management and quarrying.

Following his arrival in 1983, John Thompson Jnr served his apprenticeship across all parts of the business, working in the quarries, waste management sites and on earthworks contracts, but it was the demolition side of the business that he found the greatest excitement, and challenges.

Top: *Vehicles of the first Thompson fleet.* **Left:** *Bill Thompson with sons Billy (left) and John.* **Centre:** *The Thompson sisters, Elizabeth junior, Louise and Helen.* **Above:** *Thompsons transport depot and filling station at Prudhoe in 1970.*

the crushers that it already owned in its quarries? As the company developed and refined this, the quality was to become (as with many industry competitors) such that recycled concrete is often preferred to virgin aggregates from a practical point of view, as well as an environmental one.

With a focus on safety, training and a passionate commitment to long-term local direct employment, rather than 'hire and fire', or use agency labour, the professional management team of family and non-family members at Thompsons has maintained its reputation for hard work, value and fairness developed by Billy and John.

John Thompson Jnr led, developed and refined the demolition side of the business to become one of the UK's most prominent and respected demolition and industrial dismantling companies. He is currently the North East Regional Chairman of the National Federation of Demolition Contractors and sits on its National Executive Board.

The business has always been primarily a service company, even where that service is supplying products such as agricultural lime. Down the decades a commitment and actual practice of hard work and giving value for money has never changed.

One aspect that has changed, however, and where the company has led the way, is the promotion and use of recycled aggregate, as well as virgin aggregate, in construction projects. This came from a (self-interested) commitment to landfill avoidance. Thompsons was crushing and recycling concrete and bricks for many years before it became the norm. As it owned its own landfills – why would it fill them up with material that could be re-used as a bulk fill, if put through

Those traditions, ethos and skills are being passed on by running a demolition operative apprentice scheme, through the National Demolition Training Group, which currently has three active apprentices with a further three starting at Easter 2014.

Developing such a business has not of course been without its challenges. According to Thompsons:

"Securing the continuation of our operations (and therefore our employees' jobs) through the granting of new or extending planning permissions for our quarries and waste management facilities has been very difficult over the years, but we take on board, and often work with, local residents who think they might be affected by our

Top left: The early days at Bishop Middleham Quarry. *Top left, inset:* The first load of material out of Bishop Middleham Quarry. Pictured are driver Jim Wright and quarry manager John Purvis. *Above:* Demolition of a concrete structure above John Dobson Street in Newcastle, 1995. *Left:* John Thompson Jnr returning to the office at Prudhoe in 1998.

Billy's brother John Thompson Snr still plays an active role as Chairman of the group, whilst John Thompson Jnr and Helen Hillary (the third generation) run the business with three other Directors who are long-standing, non-family members of staff: John Burdon, Kevin Robson and Frank Hurst.

Today, demolition and dismantling (including asbestos removal) is carried out nationally, in addition to earthmoving and supplying aggregates from North Yorkshire to the Borders, and ready-mix concrete around Tyneside. Agricultural Lime is even exported to Europe thanks to the unique quality of the Lime at the Bishop Middleham quarry in Durham.

operations. No-one particularly wants to live near a quarry – but God put the stone where he did, and not under industrial estates in the main so we have to deal with that matter sensitively, but proportionately."

Clients include major construction companies, local authorities, petrochemical plants, housebuilders, commercial landlords, utility companies, power companies and industrial estate operators.

For the future the firm is planning ahead for when its permanent sites will need to be replaced. Investment in training and apprenticeships will continue whilst the company focuses on delivering a quality service to clients, and wins new ones through the consistent quality of its work.

"We have over the years faced very tough competition from national and international heavyweights, who own, or merge to form, super-quarries, but the support of our neighbours, who have seen we keep to our word, the quality of our managers, operational staff and our proven commitment to local employment and training has ensured we can maintain our aggregates business and the jobs it sustains."

One of the biggest challenges the firm faced was in April 1999 when Billy Thompson died suddenly at the age of just 59.

Meanwhile, Thompson's philosophy remains unchanged: "The aim is to finish a job, without any accidents or incidents, on time, for the price we have given, such that clients will want to invite us to tender again."

Top left: Billy Thompson (left) and John Thompson (right) pictured with office staff at their head office in 1998. ***Above left:*** Demolition of the famous 'Get Carter' multi-storey car park in 2011. ***Above right:*** A familiar sight to the people of Tyneside, a vehicle from Thompsons current fleet. ***Below:*** Thompsons of Prudhoe's head office, Princess Way, Prudhoe.

Newcastle City Library
Turning the Pages of History

Newcastle's New City Library opened on Sunday 7 June, 2009, with 5,700 visitors. Visitor numbers doubled during the opening months. On 6 November, 2009, came the Official Opening of the Library by HRH Queen Elizabeth II and Prince Philip, Duke of Edinburgh.

But the new library was only the latest manifestation of a cultural progress which had its origins more than a century earlier. The building of a city library had been first mooted as early as 1854. But not until 1874 would a Public Libraries Committee be formed, with Councillor Henry Newton as its chairman - a position he would hold until his death in 1914.

For five years there was a running argument about a site. Because the final choice in New Bridge Street, next to the Mechanics' Institute, required the demolition of the ancient Carliol Tower, a public enquiry was first necessary. Meanwhile, in September 1880, a temporary lending library was opened, occupying the ground floor of the Mechanics' Institute which was taken over by the new institution. The initial stock was 20,069 books, 2,000 of which came from the MI. With only 972

children's books, however, the age limit of members was initially restricted to those aged 14 and over.

Astonishingly, as it now seems, the books were arranged not by author, nor by subject, but by size, making it necessary to consult a catalogue to find the volume one might be looking for.

In September 1882 the central library building was finally opened.

When Newcastle's second Central Library was opened to the public in October 1968 the modern concrete building, housing some 150,000 books and public records, was rightly heralded as a great leap forward for the City.

Little could those who attended the opening ceremony of the first central library in 1882 have predicted that 86 years later there would be another opening ceremony when former Minister of Education Sir Edward Boyle would formally open a second brand new Central Library. Still less could they have anticipated that in 2009 yet a third such library would be opened by Queen Elizabeth and Prince Phillip.

Demolition of the second library began in 2007.

Many materials were recycled but the iconic 1960s Fitz Hansen chairs were repaired to be used anew. Slate from the floor of the lending library was polished and used in a new archival quality display area and the Carliol stones, which were excavated from the site of the 1880 library, were stored, ready to be displayed.

The brief was to create a building that would delight and inspire visitors. It was to be a building that made the most of technology and was to be designed to be 99% self service, freeing the library staff from processes to engage with visitors, improve access to material and provide users with an experience they would want to repeat.

The new building was to be visible, with a street frontage (something the previous library lacked). The designers wanted people to see it was a library from the street and see the building from the main shopping area. Many passers by had mistaken the 1968 building for a car park or office block. Now people are able to look inside the building and see books, displays, computers and people.

Services are no longer hidden behind closed doors. The atrium enables visitors to see most of the building from the entrance point, and scenic lifts allow them to see new areas as they move to their destinations.

Most importantly, the new building makes it possible to safely display some of the Library's hidden treasures, like the Bewick Collection and some of the rare and beautiful stock. Modern display facilities control light, temperature and relative humidity, and provide security for rare stock. This has enabled the Library to borrow material from other collections including the British Library and the House of Lords' Archive.

Over 150,000 new books were bought to add to the 100,000 in reserve book stock. And not just books: the new library also features maps, computers, music, CDs and DVDs and Wi-Fi.

But whatever building it has been housed in Newcastle's Central Library has always been, and remains, a treasure house of education, information and entertainment for Newcastle folk.

Facing page: Newcastle's original (top) and former Central Library (bottom). *This page:* Interior and exterior views of Newcastle's New City Library.

Muckle LLP
Business and Community

The law firms based in Newcastle's city centre today bear little resemblance to the small practices of a hundred years ago. Muckle LLP, based at Time Central, in Gallowgate, is a perfect example of those dramatic changes.

Yet despite those changes, the partners at Muckle are proud to have retained the ethos of the founder.

When Robert Muckle, then aged just 13, joined the solicitor's firm of JM Criddle in 1896 as an office junior, even he would never have guessed that over a century later one of the leading commercial law firms in Newcastle would bear his name. Nor that he would become Under Sheriff of Newcastle, and in 1955 be awarded the CBE.

Robert, an ambitious young man, took his articles in 1910 before qualifying as a solicitor five years later. By then the firm was known as Criddle & Criddle and based in Collingwood Street. In 1920, Robert was made a partner and the firm became Criddle, Ord & Muckle. Some years later, his son Leslie Muckle joined the partnership.

In 1951, John Hall became a partner and was responsible for moving the firm to New Bridge Street West. It was considered a bold move as the main business centre of Newcastle was then based in Collingwood Street.

The Criddles left in 1959, and the firm changed its name to Robert Muckle, Son and Hall. Robert Muckle became one of the first Newcastle lawyers to become a specialist in company law. Although the firm never opened a London branch he regularly travelled there to conduct business with southern clients.

One of Robert's clients, Wilfred Handley, was an industrial chemist based in Byker, who had invented products such as Domestos and Stergene. Robert helped Handley set up his own company and patent his products: when Handley sold out to Unilever he became a millionaire. Wilfred Handley then set up the WA Handley Charity Trust, which is still in operation today.

Today, Muckle LLP is a sharply-focused commercial firm which has a wide client base of mostly small to medium sized enterprises and corporates.

According to Stephen McNicol, Managing Partner "The firm is proactive and committed to providing an excellent service to clients. The commerciality of our lawyers ensures that the firm continues to respond rapidly to changing market conditions - exactly the same philosophy adopted by our founder Robert Muckle".

Robert Muckle was awarded his CBE for his services to the community. Today's firm is continuing his work. Stephen McNicol says, "At Muckle LLP we believe that our success and profitability must not be looked at in isolation from the wider community".

In 2002, the partners set up the Robert Muckle Charitable Fund with the Community Foundation.

Each year the firm donates a sum equal to 1% of profits to its charitable fund. Grants are made to support a wide variety of local causes. Muckle's chosen 'charity of the year' have included the NSPCC, the Heel and Toe Charity and St. Oswald's Hospice.

Its people also undertake unpaid legal work. During 2012/2013 they helped nearly 30 charities, at a notional cost of more than £100,000. In addition Muckle's people are granted up to four half days paid leave annually to undertake charitable and community work.

No wonder the firm has been a two-times recipient of a 'Heart of The Community' award for the Tyneside and Northumberland regions in the North East Business Awards, alongside professional accolades such as Regional Law Firm of the Year 2012, and Corporate Law Firm of the Year 2013 for the sixth successive year.

Elsewhere the firm's 'Green Team' continually reviews the sustainability of its business practices, calculating the firm's carbon footprint and identifying areas for improvement. That helped Muckle achieve ISO14001 accreditation, one of only a handful of UK law firms to do so.

The firm is now acknowledged as one of the region's leading commercial law firms providing businesses with first-class expert advice. Clients span the UK, plus a growing number from abroad.

Muckle cares passionately about our region, and its communities. Being a Responsible Business is

central to the firm's identity. The firm's founder Robert Muckle would have been proud of his successors' continuing adherence to his principles.

Facing page: Company founder, Robert Muckle, Under Sheriff of Newcastle upon Tyne, 1934. **Above:** The reception area of Muckle's Gallowgate premises. **Below:** Hugh Welch, Senior Partner and Stephen McNicol, Managing Partner

Jebb Metals

A Century and Half of Re-cycling

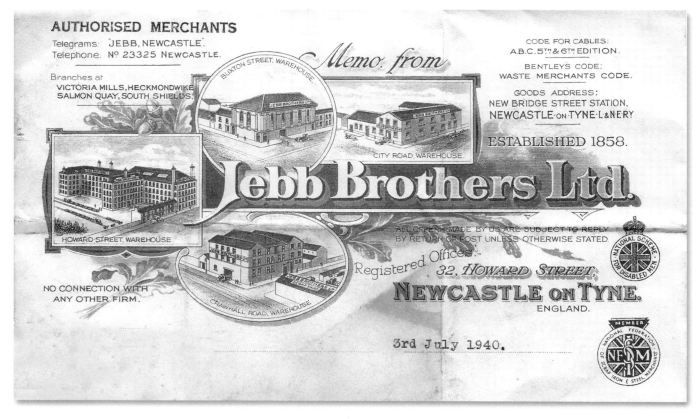

Recycling is a word very much in vogue in the 21st century. These days nothing gets thrown away – rather paper metal and glass are taken away to be reused as a matter of course. Everyone is worried about the shortage of landfill sites – or worse, that the world will run out of scarce natural resources if we don't make the best use of what we already have.

In reality recycling is as old as the hills. The Iron Age folk who once inhabited the north of England melted down broken metal items just as readily as we do today. Older readers too will readily recall the cry of the rag and bone man, his horse and cart being a common sight in Newcastle's streets not so very long ago.

These days, however, recycling is much more than just a horse and cart operation. Indeed it is big business.

And one of the most important names in the trade today is Jebb Metals.

The name Jebb has been associated with the scrap metal trade in Newcastle upon Tyne since 1860. Today Jebb Metals (Newcastle) Ltd, based in Station Road, Walker, is probably the longest established such merchant in the North East.

The story of Jebb Metals goes back to 1858 when the firm was established in Glasgow as rag merchants, handling both cottons and woollens. A few years later a few members of the Jebb family moved to Tyneside, setting up an independent business in Newcastle upon Tyne that they ran from several small buildings in the City Road area.

As the business developed so did the need for larger and more central

accommodation. By 1906 bigger premises were operating in Howard Street to cope with increased trade.

Over the following half century other branches were opened to deal with specific commodities: one in Heckmondwike, in West Yorkshire, to deal with woollen rags, and a Marine Store branch in South Shields to handle ferrous and non-ferrous scrap, ropes etc.

In the mid-1960s a brand new set of premises was built on a greenfield site: the Centurion Works at Wallsend. The totally enclosed building covered 78,000 sq ft and cost £100,000 to build. The main activities in the new building consisted of processing waste paper and non-ferrous metals.

Much of the processed materials were transported to the Chalmers Group based in Leith Scotland, of which Jebb Bros Ltd was then part of.

The present company, Jebb Metals (Newcastle) Ltd, came about as a result of a management buy-out in 1981 led by James Alexander (Alex) Kenney who until then had been the Managing Director of Jebb Bros' Metals Division by then based at Station Road, Walker. He had worked for the firm since 1968.

At the start the new operation was tiny, with just four employees. Alex's sons Philip and Stephen joined the business when they left school in 1983 and 1985 respectively.

Today, the firm employs 17 staff, and the original equipment has been replaced by powerful hydraulic shears as well as the latest hydraulic grabs and magnet cranes.

Alex officially retired in 2000 and handed over the reins to Philip and Stephen, though he still came in every day to lend a hand before sadly passing away in 2008.

Though clients were initially all from the UK, today recycled metal is a worldwide business with the firm exporting to Europe, India and China.

The firm's long experience and knowledge allows it to buy all grades of non-ferrous metals such as brass, copper, lead and aluminium and other alloys such as stainless steels, then process and grade them to customers' requirements for melting at foundries both in the UK and overseas.

Jebb Metals also handle significant tonnages of ferrous metals such as light steel cuttings, steel punchings, profile plate etc, which are also processed to customers' requirements and sent to iron foundries and steel works.

As for the future, as the world's natural resources get scarcer, and competition for them gets ever fiercer, the demand for recycled metals can only increase. The rag and bone man may be history, but recycling on an industrial scale is the future. Today, Jebb Metals (Newcastle) Ltd is in position to lead the pack in an ever-expanding business.

Top left, facing page: A Jebb Brothers Ltd letterhead from 1940. *Bottom, facing page:* The Centurion Works office block which housed the admin side of the business. *Top left and centre:* 1965 views inside the waste paper warehouse. *Top right:* The non-ferrous metal warehouse in 1965. *Below:* A Jebb Metals company vehicle.

Eldon Square
The Centre of Shopping

Eldon Square is the heart of shopping in Newcastle featuring an impressive list of high street names including Debenhams, Fenwick, John Lewis and Marks & Spencer, world famous brands including Apple, Superdry and Hollister and flagship stores for New Look, River Island and Topshop. There's a fine choice of cafés and restaurants including Boost Juice Bars, Nando's, Pizza Express, Starbucks Coffee, Strada, Wagamama and more.

incorporating apartments, offices, leisure facilities, car parking, a bus concourse and a new market hall as well as 976,000 square feet of shops. Work on the Centre began in 1973 to the design of architects Chapman Taylor Partners at a cost of £60 million, creating the largest covered shopping centre in Britain.

Opened by the Queen in 1977, 40% was owned by the Council and the remainder split between the Shell Pension Trust and CSC Plc - Capital Shopping Centres. It covered an area of almost ten acres,

Popular celebrities visiting Eldon Square have included many well-known people, including Muhammad Ali and Bjorn Borg as well as Her Majesty Queen Elizabeth, the late Queen Mother

With refurbishment and development of Eldon Square in 1988 and 1989, an extra 80,000 square feet on the south side of the Centre was created, the new Newgate Mall incorporating a Food Court. More shops and a link to the south end of the city followed in 1990.

Shell's interest in the Centre was bought out by CSC in 2005.

The first phase of the Eldon Square West development in 2006, provided an additional 22,000 sq ft of space on Blackettbridge mall for retailers including Carphone Warehouse, Quiz, Esquires Coffee, Holland & Barratt, Officers Club, and Trespass. Two new restaurants, Strada and Wagamama, brought new vitality to the area.

Top: An early view of Eldon Square. *Left:* Construction of Eldon Square Shopping Centre. *Circled:* The official opening by the Queen in her Silver Jubilee year, 1977. *Above:* An early view of Eldon Square, with the distinctive mushroom shaped café.

In 2007 a new £11 million bus terminal opened between John Lewis and the historic Haymarket bus station.

Eldon Square - St George's Way Mall - completed in February 2008, offered 14 new shops comprising 48,000 sq ft of space and created a link from the new bus interchange. Stores in the new mall included Argos Extra, Boots, John Lewis, Starbucks Coffee, Serendipity, Esquires Coffee, Oil & Vinegar, Nando's and Waitrose.

Later that same year Newcastle City Council transformed Old Eldon Square, landscaping it with new grass, flowerbeds, trees, shrubberies, walkways, seating and lighting. At the heart of the square, Newcastle's war memorial, fully restored by CSC, was overlooked by new restaurants Strada, Wagamama and Nando's.

Eldon Square South (St Andrew's Way Mall) was completed in February 2010. Some 30,000 tonnes of concrete and brickwork was crushed and reused in the new construction. The new mall included a 'green' roof: within a week it was housing a family of bats!

The 410,000 sq ft mall is anchored by a four-storey flagship Debenhams and houses retailers such as River Island, New Look and Topshop. Popular high street names, including Tesco Metro, Burton, Dorothy Perkins, Miss Selfridge, Schuh and Paperchase also feature. New retailers to the centre included Hollister, Superdry, All Saints and Oasis as well as the only Apple Store between Sheffield and Glasgow.

His Royal Highness Prince Richard, The Duke of Gloucester, officially opened St Andrew's Way in July 2010.

Eldon Square had become one of the largest city centre shopping centres in the UK, occupying 1.35m sq ft with 151 stores. By December 2010 annual footfall had risen from 29 million shoppers in 2009 to 34 million.

Work began on more development in January 2013, with £22m invested in further modernisation, including rebuilding and extending the Northumberland Street entrance.

Main shareholder CSC changed its name to intu properties plc in 2013. The change coincided with the introduction of increased opportunities for e-commerce.

Next is a £17 million dining quarter which will incorporate the Grade II listed facades and views over Old Eldon Square, Greys Monument and the Grainger Town Conservation Area. It is expected to open in 2015.

A whole generation has now grown up knowing no other cityscape than the one that contains the Eldon Square Shopping Centre. Millions of visitors have passed through its doors since its opening. Some 70,000 a year come from Scandinavia, so famous is Newcastle as the place to shop. Eldon Square has become an iconic part of the city.

This page: Recent views of intu Eldon Square, the heart of shopping in Newcastle.

Abbeyfield

Making a Difference to the Lives of the Elderly in Newcastle

Choosing where and how you live when you're older is one of life's major decisions. Abbeyfield is a charity that provides housing, support and care for people at different stages of later life. It is a not-for-profit organisation with one mission: to enhance the quality of life for older people by making their lives easier and more fulfilling.

When Richard Carr-Gomm became Britain's first male home-help in 1956 he was shocked at the isolation and loneliness of some of the older people he visited.

The former officer in the Coldstream Guards spent his £250 Army gratuity as a deposit to buy a small house in Bermondsey, South London, and invited two local residents who had been living alone, to join him. The first Abbeyfield house was born.

Soon more people were invited to live in the house. Like-minded volunteers (not least his future wife, Susan Gibbs) joined Richard in caring for, and improving the lives of, older people who had been living without friendship or support. Several people started fundraising and donating money to help Richard and his team continue their work. Within two years there were six houses and 26 residents.

But Richard wasn't satisfied. By the end of 1960 he had helped to create new societies in eight other London boroughs. And the charity had spread to 15 places outside the capital, through the groundbreaking efforts of volunteers.

By the mid-1960s Abbeyfield's ethos had spread to Newcastle upon Tyne. Private residences around the city were acquired to provide sheltered accommodation, meals and companionship for people living alone.

In 1970, Abbeyfield purchased its largest house - The Grove in Gosforth, the magnificent former family residence of Samuel Smith, the founder of the famous Ringtons Tea company, and later one of the owner's of Kemsley Newspapers. The house had been in the hands of the Samares Trust since 1949, providing a home for ladies who had found themselves living in reduced circumstances — many due to the war.

Top left: *An image of The Grove when it was a private residence.* ***Left:*** *The construction of the garden room at Thorney Close in 1991.* ***Above:*** *Residents enjoying each other's company at Castle Farm.*

Philanthropists continued to donate to Abbeyfield. One house, the splendid Thorney Close in Fenham, was donated in 1991 by the late Marjorie Lawson - a well known philanthropist in the west end of the city. The house continues today to provide supported living, home-cooked hot meals and much needed companionship for six elderly residents.

The changing needs of elderly people subsequently led to a change in provision – Abbeyfield Newcastle upon Tyne now runs four homes in the area; The Grove and Castle Farm – both in Gosforth – provide residential care home facilities for the elderly, and Linden Road in Gosforth and Thorney Close in Fenham offer supported sheltered accommodation.

All four homes have an annual tea party where they invite neighbours to join them in order to ensure that anyone who is lonely in the neighbourhood knows there are friends nearby.

Meanwhile, just as was the case when Abbeyfield first began, Abbeyfield in Newcastle has an army of volunteers working alongside a team of professional paid staff. It is these volunteers that make Abbeyfield so different from other care providers. The volunteers come from varying backgrounds and, whether they go and spend an hour with residents over coffee, or take them out to the shops or to their doctors' appointments, they make a huge difference to the lives of the Abbeyfield family.

Thanks to the hard work and dedication of staff, and the ever growing team of volunteers working across the four properties, Abbeyfield Newcastle achieved the organisation's Gold Star Award in 2013.

Founder Richard Carr-Gomm was awarded the OBE in 1985. He died in 2008.

Today, Abbeyfield runs 700 sheltered houses in the UK, and 80 homes for those too frail to take care of themselves, providing accommodation for more than 8,000 people

Abbeyfield has, however, grown to be not just a British organisation but a global charity, providing accommodation and services in 15 countries across seven continents.

Top: A garden party for residents across all Abbeyfield houses. *Above:* Peter Fryer, Abbeyfield Newcastle's longest serving volunteer receiving his award for 47 years of service. *Below left:* The opening of Castle Farm which was purpose-built in 1993 on the back of the demand for Abbeyfield accommodation across the city. *Below:* A recent view of Castle Farm.

Parkland Engineering
Industrial Hose Specialists

Formed in 1978 as a distributor of industrial hose and fittings to Tyneside, Parkland Engineering Ltd, based on the North Tyne Industrial Estate, Benton, now supplies the whole UK market and many countries throughout Europe, and China.

With branches in Aberdeen, Glasgow, Teesside, Carlisle and Newcastle, plus a sales office in Preston, the firm supplies a full range of industrial, hydraulic, metallic, PTFE and silicone hose assemblies. To complement the Parkland-manufactured hose range the company also has an online range of over 60,000 engineering products.

At the outset, the firm consisted of two partners, Doug Sutherland and Barry Parker. The company name simply took the 'Park' from Parker and the 'land' from Sutherland. On the very first day the partners hit the road with nothing but a set of trade directories. "How long have you been in business" the first prospective client asked – "About two hours" came the honest reply – "but try us and you'll soon find that we are very competitive".

Doug's unpaid wife, Shirley, never left the house between 8am and 5pm Monday to Friday in order to take phone calls. The partners phoned in from telephone boxes every hour to pick up messages.

Much of the early business was from ship builders and ship repair yards, and from work on the new Tyne Tunnel and the tunnel between Keilder and Teesside.

One very big job for Middle Docks involved cutting a large ship in half lengthways, and inserting an extra deck between the lower and upper halves. Apart from supplying hose Parkland also supplied thousands of worm drive clips to fasten electrical cables.

The firm's first warehouse – 1,400 sq ft in the 250-year-old old Maling Pottery building was unmanned. Doug and Barry would dash in to take deliveries, make up orders and then deliver them. The warehouse 'office' was made from the sides of tea chests.

First decision was to pull the old office down and build something more substantial: when the first section was removed the whole thing collapsed and an enormous cloud of soot, accumulated over the previous 200 years, erupted.

*Top left: Doug Sutherland in the early years. **Above Centre:** Some of the products supplied by Parkland. **Below left:** As manufacturers of custom built shaped and straight hoses Parkland are uniquely positioned to design and manufacture a hose to customers precise requirements. **Below:** A view inside the company's fully-stocked warehouse.*

Shirley did not get out the way quickly enough, and she emerged from the cloud blackened from head to toe.

There was certainly no time for airs and graces. One evening as Doug and Shirley were leaving home to attend a dinner dance they received a call to make an urgent delivery to Reyrolles. The pair went to the warehouse, packed the goods, and then carried the box the full length of the Reyrolles factory – Shirley in her long evening dress and Doug in his dinner suit: they were cheered all the way!

In the 1980s, growth was the order of the day. In 1985, the firm bought Corrance & Yuill Ltd of Glasgow, the largest distributor of Dunlop industrial hose in Scotland. The following year a 50% share was also acquired in a small Carlisle company.

Manufacturing of shaped industrial rubber hoses began in 1987.

Manufacturing capacity increased by 50% in 1994 when the business moved to a larger site in Newcastle. Parkland ISO 9001 & 14001 accredited are now a key supplier to many household name original equipment manufacturers around Europe.

.

The acquisition of Acorn Precision Engineering in 1997 enabled in-house manufacture of tooling for hose.

Acquisitions continued apace in 2000 when Fluid Instruments was bought from liquidators in order to expand the Teesside operation which had opened in 1999.

A branch was opened in Aberdeen in 2005. Two years later larger premises were needed there to handle increased turnover after the acquisition of the hose business of Aberdeen-based K&L Ross. Larger premises were bought in Newcastle in 2006. By 2010 a fire industry specialist had been recruited to sell a unique range of high pressure rubber fire hose and couplings designed by Doug Sutherland, for which design registration has been obtained. A new filter assembly for the Fire and Rescue Services was designed and patented in 2012.

Larger premises were purchased in Teesside in 2012.

Most recently, in 2013, the company acquired the remaining 50% of shares in the Carlisle company Border Hydraulics & Pneumatics, completing the process which had begun in 1986.

Today, now in his eighties, Doug Sutherland still enjoys working a five day week – surely the longest serving member of the UK's hose industry.

Top left: *On-site testing by Parkland's National Hose Managements Service which provides valuable hose testing and certification services across the UK.* **Left:** *Some of the team outside the Newcastle factory.* **Above:** *Doug at 80 "Chairing" a Managers meeting at the Teesside premises.* **Below:** *Parkland Engineering's Newcastle premises.*

John Lewis
60 years in Newcastle

n 2013 John Lewis Newcastle celebrated its 60th year as part of the John Lewis Partnership.

For longer than any reader can possibly recall the centre of Newcastle has been famed for the quality of its shops. Of course, there have been, and still are, many different kinds of retail premises. There are many small family-owned businesses trading alongside huge chain stores representing nationally renowned firms. But as we all learned in our schooldays mighty oaks grow from tiny acorns. Some of today's small businesses may themselves grow to become famous chains. And equally some of today's mighty commercial giants, not least John Lewis', started their lives as small businesses run by one man.

Today, the John Lewis Partnership is one of Britain's leading retail businesses. Surprisingly to those not in the know, the business belongs to all those who work within it on a permanent basis; those staff are known as 'partners' from the day they join. The firm has no outside shareholders: all the ordinary share capital is held by John Lewis Trustees on behalf of all the partners, who in turn each get a share of any profits made each year as well as a say in how the business is run.

The John Lewis story really began in 1864. The original, eponymous John Lewis, then a young draper from Somerset, had arrived in London in 1856 with just a single golden guinea (£1.05) in his pocket. He opened a small draper's shop which he developed into a department store, located, as it still is today, in London's Oxford Street. The first day's takings amounted to just one pound. Success came gradually, but John Lewis gained a reputation for honesty and for having the largest selection of goods in the West End. In 1905, John Lewis also bought the Peter Jones department store in Sloane Square to expand the business. John Lewis had two sons, Spedan and Oswald: on his sons' twenty-first birthdays he gave each of them a quarter share in the business,

Top left: *John Lewis, founder of an empire.* **Left:** *Bainbridge's store decorated for the coronation of King George VI in 1937.* **Above:** *Interior of Bainbridges in the 1970s.*

To mark the 60th anniversary, John Lewis Newcastle has created a memory wall, located in the Espresso Bar on the first floor, where customers can see how the shop evolved over the previous 60 years. Visitors to the exhibition can also share their earliest or favourite memories of shopping at John Lewis Newcastle in a special memory book.

Isabella Miller, Managing Director of John Lewis Newcastle, says: "Celebrating the shop's 60th anniversary has been exciting not only for our Partners but our customers too and we have had a fantastic reaction to our memory wall and book. John Lewis Newcastle is steeped in history dating back to the 19th century and it's fantastic to see that the world's first department store is still thriving to this day."

Spedan Lewis became sole owner in 1928. The following year he signed a deed of settlement which transferred shares in the business to trustees. The profits would henceforth be distributed to employees.

In 1953, the John Lewis Partnership took over the famous Bainbridge of Newcastle store, founded in 1838 by Emerson Muschamp Bainbridge. Reputed to be the world's first department store, the shop continued to trade as Bainbridge until 2002 when the name officially changed to John Lewis Newcastle.

Today, the John Lewis Partnership operates 39 John Lewis shops across the UK (30 department stores and nine John Lewis At Home), as well as related internet businesses, and 295 Waitrose shops in the UK and abroad. The business has annual gross sales of over £9.5bn. It is the UK's largest example of worker co-ownership in which all 84,700 staff are Partners in the business.

At John Lewis value is about more than price, it's also shown in the quality of the products and an expert, highly professional service. Partners keep a close eye on competitors to ensure they always offer great quality at fair prices, supported by excellent service and, as a result, John Lewis provides value that's unrivalled on the high street. The Partners' commitment to the business' success is reflected in the impartial advice and excellent after-sales support provided. 'Never Knowingly Undersold' has been John Lewis' trading philosophy since 1925, and that remains at the very heart of everything it does.

Top left: *Market Street's Christmas windows in 1971.* **Left:** *An exterior shot of the store during official opening of the Eldon Square Centre in 1976.* **Above:** *Newcastle's John Lewis store.*

Newcastle Building Society
Local Knowledge, Mutual Understanding

By 1920, the Society's assets stood at £1 million, and by 1928, had doubled. In 1942, the North Eastern Building Society transferred its assets to the Newcastle upon Tyne Permanent Building Society; it was followed by the Portland Building Society in 1961 and the St. Andrews Building Society in 1979.

John Heppell had become Secretary of the Society in 1888 and his son, P. Forsyth Heppell, was elected Chairman in 1945. In turn, his son, P.W.E. Heppell, became Chairman from 1966 until 1987, by which time his son, J.W. Heppell had already joined the board.

Another substantial figure was Tom Bathurst. He became Chief Executive in 1960.

Today, Newcastle Building Society is the biggest building society in the North East. It is the eighth largest in the UK, with assets of more than £4.4 billion.

The Grainger Permanent Building Society, established in 1863 in Westgate Road, Newcastle, lent £22,177 in its first year. The name was chosen to perpetuate the memory of the well-known Newcastle developer, Richard Grainger.

After the Second World War the assets of the Society had increased to £2 million. During that conflict, the Society had taken over the City of Newcastle Building Society, and, within a year of the ending of hostilities, had also taken over the Northumberland Building Society.

In 1957, the Grainger merged with the Percy Building Society, establishing a society with assets of £7 million. In 1974, the Victory Building Society of South Shields was also absorbed. A year later the Society changed its name to The Grainger Building Society.

The Newcastle upon Tyne Permanent Building Society (NPBS) was established in 1861 by George Brewis and Thomas Strachan with the aim 'by mutual co-operation to enable the members to acquire property and to supply to the saving classes a safe means of realising a good interest'. However, ten years passed before the Society opened permanent offices in Central Buildings, Grainger Street West.

A branch was established in Carlisle in 1961. In the early 1970s, the Society installed its first computer at a cost of £1 million.

At the end of 1980, the Society amalgamated with the Grainger Building Society to form the Newcastle Building Society. Tom Bathurst became Joint Chief Executive alongside the former Chief Executive of the Grainger. Bill Midgley became Chief Executive in 1986.

Top left: An interest calculating digital accounting machine used in the early 1960s. Above: Grainger & Percy Building Society Literature from the late 50s and early 60s. Below: The Hood Street Banking Hall in 1958.

Following Bill Midgley's retirement in 1998, Robert Hollinshead became Chief Executive. He was instrumental in the development of the Society's technology systems.

In 1991, the Society acquired the old BBC Broadcasting House at 54, New Bridge Street for its headquarters. After three years work the building, re-named Portland House, was officially opened in November 1994 by HRH Princess Margaret.

The old building at the centre of Portland House, built in 1826, began life as the Newcastle Maternity Hospital.

In 1992, The Newcastle Building Society saw its assets pass the £1 billion mark, and its branches became electronically linked to Head Office.

The Newcastle developed a system of 'virtualisation' in 2002, enabling it to utilise staff anywhere in the Society's network, regardless of location.

In 1992, The Newcastle Building Society Community Fund was set up, with over £100,000 distributed each year. The objectives of the fund are to promote training and learning, to nurture and encourage new talent, and to improve the quality of life in local communities.

The Society launched a diversified core product offering known as Solutions in 1997. This business focuses on providing outsourced financial services to other financial institutions. It is now regarded by many as the market-leader in its field.

Colin Seccombe became Chief Executive in 2006.

December 2006 saw the merger of The Newcastle Building Society and The Universal Building Society. This heralded the opening of a new office for the Society at Cobalt Business Park.

In 2010 a New Chief Executive was appointed; Jim Willens, who brought more than 25 years worth of experience of the building society sector. The same year saw the opening of a new style flagship branch for the Society on Northumberland Street.

The Society's Charity of the Year programme, which aims to support one charity locally over a 12 month period, was launched in 2008. All money is raised by staff: more than £100k has now been donated.

The Society launched its popular Sir Bobby Robson Foundation charity-linked ISA and Saver in 2010. It donates an extra percentage of interest to the Foundation. More than £500k has now been raised.

a new brand image and slogan was adopted in 2013 to emphasise the key points of difference: 'Local Knowledge. Mutual Understanding.'

After 150 years The Newcastle Building Society continues to be a local Society for local people. The Newcastle is committed to remaining a mutual building society, and being a trusted provider of financial services.

Top left: A bird's eye view of Portland House. **Left:** The Society's Cobalt Business Park offices. **Centre:** Staff and some of the winners pictured at the Society's Cornerstone Teesside awards in 2013. **Above:** The launch of Newcastle Building Society's relationship with the Sir Bobby Robson Foundation. Pictured are Sir Bobby's widow, Lady Elsie Robson and Jim Willens, Newcastle Building Society's Chief Executive.

ACKNOWLEDGMENTS

THE PUBLISHERS WOULD LIKE TO THANK THE FOLLOWING

FOR THEIR HELP IN MAKING PHOTOGRAPHS AVAILABLE FOR THIS BOOK

NEWCASTLE CITY LIBRARY – ANGELA FORSTER & SARAH MULLIGAN

WIKIMEDIA COMMONS

TYNE & WEAR, THE COMMONS

MIRRORPIX